Recovering Reality

"Freedom from the torment of addiction"

By
ERIK FREDERICKSON
www.RecoveringReality.com

Editor: Brae Wyckoff
Assistant Editor: Kristine Frederickson
Cover art by GetCovers

Scripture quotations are taken from the Amplified® Bible (**AMP**), Copyright © 2015 by The Lockman Foundation Used by permission. www.Lockman.org

Scripture quotations marked (**ESV**) are from The ESV® Bible (The Holy Bible, English Standard Version®), copyright © 2001 by Crossway, a publishing ministry of Good News Publishers. Used by permission. All rights reserved.

Recovering Reality

"Freedom from the torment of addiction"

Contents

Endorsements

"People struggling with substance abuse confront difficult days of utter despair, lacking the desire to get better. Uplifting stories of those beating the battle of addiction can help sway someone from making the wrong choice and aid in pulling themselves from that deep hole of darkness. Erik, through his book, gives you full access into his dark maze but also finds the beauty in God's Grace. He exemplifies heart, sacrifice (investment), and how to deal with both emotional and physical pain. He lets the pain subside and feels its void with love, passion, power, and purpose. I recommend this book to anyone looking for hope and the intestinal fortitude to pave a new life in their recovery journey."

-Dr. Chambless R. Johnston III
-Addictionologist and Founder of New Life Medicine

"The insights from this book will prove to be life-changing for those who encounter it, whether it be individuals who want freedom for themselves or loved ones who are looking for hope. Erik has helped lead thousands into freedom from addiction, and this book will assuredly help readers to jumpstart that journey."

-Austin Kamban
- Kamban Music - Recovery Advocate

"Recovery is such a roller coaster ride for everyone involved, with a lot of apprehensions during the up times and hopelessness during the down times. Erik's story is as brutally honest as you can be, but most books on addiction and recovery stop there. Erik's story is the journey out of the bondage of addiction and the bondage of managing addiction. You CAN be fully transformed so that returning to the past isn't even an option anymore because that person and their struggles no longer exist."

-Paul Dabdoub
- CEO of Life Coach Training Institute

"I'm so grateful for Erik Frederickson's courage to tell his story in such a raw, real, and relatable way. He takes the reader through the gateway emotions and challenges of a young boy, the pitfalls of addiction, and how those ultimately lead him to the "end of his rope" as a young man. Erik demonstrates the life-changing effectiveness of literally renewing our minds and understanding how the mind, body, and spirit work together to bring healing and restoration. He is a walking miracle and testimony of God's goodness. You will be encouraged to run your race and live fully alive!"

-JENN KAUTSCH,
author of "Look Alive, Sis," founder and visionary of SoberSis.com

"Erik's journey is a true testament to the power of resilience and determination. Once trapped in the clutches of addiction, Erik takes us on his journey to discover the strength within him to face his demons head-on and reclaim his life. Despite setbacks and temptations, Erik remained steadfast in his commitment to sobriety. Over time, Erik's transformation became visible to all. He rebuilt broken relationships, mended trust, and became a pillar of support for others battling addiction. His story has become an inspiration, giving hope to those who thought recovery was impossible. Today, Erik continues to live a fulfilling life, free from the chains of addiction. He serves as a beacon of hope, sharing his story and offering guidance to those who are still fighting their own battles. Erik's journey reminds us that with determination, support, and a spiritual awakening, anyone can overcome addiction and embrace a brighter future."

-Alika Gambill
- Founder of Pro Recovery Power

"Erik truly understands God's heart of redemption!"

-John Huffman, CEO of Huffman
Construction and Pastor of Harvest Recovery Ministries

"First, not only do I endorse Erik's book, but I highly recommend everyone gets a copy. Not only did I relate to the addiction side of it. I myself was entangled in a love affair with opioids, which led me to Jails, Institutions, and even Death. But now, because of God's love, so many prayers, and my surrender, I, too, am now in a place like Erik. I am helping and serving others to get to the place of knowing their identities as children of God and breaking the vicious cycle of addiction for generations to come. As I read Erik's content, there was so much I related to because of my past. But what I really loved was all the content material about what exactly we are dealing with when it comes to understanding opioids and addictions. And how we can go about defeating them. Through my fellowship with the Lord, I once said to him, "Lord, someone needs to write a book like this for more understanding of what we are dealing with and how to help." And Erik has done it! I was blessed with "Hope" as I read this, and I know you will be too."

-Recovery Pastor Bradley Fields,
LifeWay Church - NP

"Erik's radical journey helps us see our own lives from the lenses of Heaven as he shares the darkness he walked through to find freedom. His book helped me see my own story in a new way and reminded me that anything is possible with God."

-Mark Gagarin
- Recovery Pastor - Awaken Church

"I had the privilege of meeting Erik a few years ago when he contacted me to be on his Recovering Reality Podcast. Erik has a powerful story of overcoming that needs to be heard. I strongly feel his story will help many who have been affected by addiction. We live in a world that is filled with people desperately searching for answers on how to get free from addiction. I believe Erik's book will do just that and be an additional resource to the coaching he offers. As I was reading his book, I couldn't stop thinking of the young people it will impact. It will even be a source of encouragement to parents who lay in bed at night worrying about their children. This book will touch the lives of many."

-Paula Jauch -founder and CEO of Walking Into Freedom, a nonprofit, trauma survivor, speaker, and 2x award-winning author of *Cross Addicted: Breaking Free of Family Trauma and Addiction*

"When I moved to a new state and became the leader of an addiction recovery program, a now mutual friend said, 'You really need to meet Erik Frederickson.' He was right. Erik is inspiring. Authentic. And relentless in his pursuit to know Jesus and work with him to set others free. You'll see that in his story, and you'll be introduced to true freedom. If you're bound in addiction or know someone who is, I also say to you, 'You really need to meet Erik Frederickson.'"

-Will Kitchen, Executive Director,
Teen Challenge Southeast - Fort Myers

"Erik reveals the dark patterns that suck people into addiction with vivid detail, but he doesn't stop there. He also reveals the blueprint to freedom from addiction through Jesus."

-Jodi Salvo
-Director of Substance Use Prevention, OhioGuidestone

Acknowledgments

RⁱR

JESUS, WHAT A crazy journey we've been on. I was a tormented, lost, and broken man when you stepped onto the scene of my life, and you saw my potential and value. I'll try and show my gratitude to you through my life lived for the remainder of my days. I love you, thank you for life and life more abundantly.

My beautiful wife, Mayana, you are my best friend and Mi Bonita. When we met, I didn't have two dimes to rub together, and you loved me and followed Jesus with me on this wild adventure. I love you, thank you for being you. Lucas, Liam, and Logan, you boys are gifts from heaven. I pray I can be the dad you deserve all the days of my life. I love you, boys!

Mom, thanks for never giving up on me, even when you had every right to. And thank you for helping me with my book. Love you. To my dad, brothers, and sisters, thank you for your friendship and love. Thank you for letting me back into your lives after all my years of darkness.

Paul Dabdoub, thank you for investing in my life. I wouldn't be where I am without your friendship. Love you, my friend.

Brae and Jill Wyckoff, thank you for how you live and your friendship. I love you guys.

To our church family at Destiny Church Naples, we love you and are very grateful to be a part of what He is doing in our midst. Thank you for your love for God and people. I wouldn't be where I am today without the help and encouragement of many others. Thank you if you've ever sowed into my life in any way.

CHAPTER 1
The Beginning

I T HAD BEEN a long and paranoid drive. My mind was juggling three different pinball games, and the only certain thing was that my future was completely uncertain.

Although that drive was riddled with fear and anxiety, it was nothing compared to the nightmarish thirteen years of drug and alcohol addiction that I had lived through. Up to this point in my journey, I had watched over thirty friends die in one way or another from addiction. I was no different than them. I was slowly dying, trapped in the middle of that lonely and dark vortex. I was desperate for this living nightmare to be over. I was out of options, out of bridges to burn, and out of energy to keep chasing the dark and twisted fantasy of addiction.

This particular escape route was a drive back home to my parent's house at the age of twenty-six with nothing but a long list of overwhelming problems and addictions. I had again agreed to go to treatment for the second time. I had been drinking myself to death in a small town in southern Utah. The only reason I wasn't doing drugs at that time was that alcohol was easier to get and more effective at numbing my pain.

How did I get here?

I had no license, no insurance, no registration, and a handful of warrants out for my arrest as the two-and-a-half-hour drive back to my parents' house stirred up my thick and intense anxiety.

As I pondered what treatment would be like this time, I recalled the unwanted and humbling phone call I made to my parents as I asked for help to try and get into another rehab program. They agreed. They always wanted to help whenever I showed signs of truly desiring to change my life. I was ready to face this mess, and the first step was driving to my parent's house.

The uncomfortable arrival was near as I pulled off the freeway toward their house. I had spent many years driving the backroads of their city avoiding the police, so I figured it would be a safe bet for the last five minutes of the journey to take the back roads.

I pulled off the freeway and turned my car down a back road, and it just so happened that a cop turned right behind me. Would you imagine that? Fear gripped me, and a shot of adrenaline coursed through my veins. I thought I'd nonchalantly speed up and try to make a quick turn, hoping the police officer wouldn't see my expired tags. He must have noticed my unusual acceleration, and those daunting blue and red flashing lights lit up behind me. I knew it was over.

I pulled over on the quiet back streets of middle-class suburbia and instantly started chain-smoking cigarettes. I knew I was going to jail, and there was no smoking in that cement cage: this wasn't my first rodeo. There was something different about this time; it was as if time reached a slow crawl, and I knew it was best to admit defeat.

I had had enough. I was done. As the officer approached the window, I was already waving the white flag of surrender. The flashing lights, the uniformed officer with his badge and gun, and the flood of past arrest memories raced through my mind. Before he could ask for my license, registration, and insurance (I knew the drill all too well), I had made up my mind.

He came to my window, and I handed him my license and said, "Here you go. I have no license, registration, or insurance, and I have a handful of warrants out for my arrest."

He looked at me and said, "Okay, just wait here and sit tight." As another squad car pulled on the scene, my mind entered an unusual moment of clarity. The racing thoughts slowed, and a foreign internal shift began. I knew a power bigger than me would be needed to escape this mess. I had asked God for help many times before, but something felt different about this episode. Until now, I didn't know who God was, nor did I want a relationship with Him. I just wanted Him to fix my problems.

I thought to myself, "I'm heading to my parents to get help. I'm completely defeated, I'm beyond tired, and I'm out of options. God, help me." I'm confident that the length and eloquence of my prayer didn't rouse God's heart. I believe it was the posture of my heart that moved God's heart. I was honest and sincere. I couldn't do it anymore. I surrendered.

Wait...

Wait, surrender? Why now? Why is this time different?

Before we get to the good part of my life and the radical transformation that has taken place, you'll need to hear the whole story. So, let's go on a journey. My journey may differ from yours, but I believe we are more alike than you think.

Thirteen years before this moment...

It was a hot summer day.

CHAPTER 2
The Encounter

RR

THE TEMPERATURE WAS in the mid-eighties, inching towards the nineties in upper-middle-class suburbia in Orem, Utah. As was the standard on Sunday mornings, my family and I, along with just about everyone else in Utah County, were focused on attending the local Mormon Church.

Sundays in Utah County have an almost ghost town feel, as more than eighty percent of the more than half a million population of the county congregate at their local church building for three hours of structured devotion.

The specifically designed Mormon Church buildings are very noticeable, with their sharp steeples on street corners about every four or five blocks apart. The Mormon religion is the lifestyle there, and nearly everyone in that culture does nothing on Sundays but attend church and family dinners.

The stores shut down. The roads have far fewer people on them. Then, there's a mass exodus from the local Church house every three hours.

This Sunday, I, along with my large family of seven (at that time), hurried to the church building only a few blocks away from our six-bedroom house. I was fourteen and not too enthusiastic about attending church every Sunday. But as is typical in Mormon culture, you don't have much choice when you're young and born into it.

It was always a small and entertaining circus—getting all five kids ready and on time to service—let alone smiling and in the first few rows of the sanctuary. With three older sisters, myself, and one younger brother, you can imagine how steering this ship on time to its rightful destination had its challenges. Teenage girls with clothing and makeup issues, and the two of us younger boys wondered why it always took so long for the girls to get ready.

We would make our way out the door, most often walking to church, unless it was winter. I liked walking, even if it was cold out. It made it easier for me to leave the church and head home at the moment of freedom. That is, if I hadn't tried to slip out unnoticed before service was officially over.

I wore my white button-up shirt, tie, and slacks on this memorable day. A suit and tie and, most often, a clean-shaven face is the proto-typical uniform of the devout Mormon. Buttoning the last button on that white shirt always felt like I was choking myself into submission for the three-hour attention span that the church services required.

Walking to church, I passed the two-story homes along the way. Neatly-kept yards and clean sidewalks filled this suburban neigh-borhood. Mt. Timpanogos and Mt. Cascade were the backdrop of this conservative and devoutly religious area. Ground level in Orem is an elevation of nearly five thousand feet, soaring to roughly twelve thousand feet at the peaks of the two towering mountains.

I stared at the ground, dressed in my Sunday best, as minivans and SUVs packed with large families rolled past. Sweat started to show under my collar when I reached the church. It was only a short journey from our house. A strange nervousness came upon me that day.

On this day, we somehow all made it on time. As was standard procedure for Mormon Church services, we began with a welcome and someone offering a prayer from the pulpit. Then, we all sang hymns accompanied most often by a woman at the piano—hymns often written in the 1800s or early 1900s. I didn't get it, but I pretended to sing to spare myself the silent look from others, "Why aren't you singing!?" So, I sang quietly. I am not one to carry a tune, so I didn't want anyone to hear my inharmonious and unenthusiastic words. It was more lip movement than actual singing.

As I sunk into the meeting's religious order, my mind drifted. I had no idea this seemingly ordinary moment was about to turn into an extraordinary and life-defining mark in a snap of the fingers.

There I was, sitting on the third row of the church pews. A spiritual experience was about to mysteriously unveil itself to me. It wasn't a religious experience. I had had plenty of those.

During this period, a shift in direction synergistically began exhibiting itself. Having been born and raised in Los Gatos and Campbell, California for the first ten years, we moved to Utah when I was around ten. My parents felt impressed to move to Utah, and my father was able to transfer to a branch of his company there. Also, my family are devout Mormons, and, in many ways, it is easier to practice this religion in Utah County. This demographic change in our natural world unknowingly stirred a change in my spiritual world—but I would not have been able to explain any of this at the time.

I was also starting to act out. I wasn't sure why, but my irritation had begun playing out through my words and actions. After living in Utah for a few years, these behaviors came to a slow boil. I started carrying a chip on my shoulder and felt like *I had to prove something to the world around me.* This internal struggle had me seeking external comfort, and I had begun to seek acceptance from the kids who were looked at as the cool kids. It just so happened that most kids that people thought were cool were also making trouble and experimenting with drugs and alcohol.

I was slowly making this crowd of hooligans my choice of friends, and the same inevitable problems in their lives started showing up in mine. It was a period of confusion, but as with most people who are confused, I thought I had perfect clarity into what was going on.

This regimented and strictly structured Mormon church culture was forcing my internal issues to surface, and I almost unknowingly began to dislike life. Sundays were the days I dreaded most, and truthfully, it wasn't outside the norm for me to be hungover from the shenanigans that took place the night before.

This Sunday, a day of significant meaning, I was tired and distant-minded. Little did I know my life was about to change dramatically. I can recall no special moment in the church service that caused me to pause and ponder. No one laid hands on me to pray and invoke a spiritual event. Everything was going according to normal when, out of nowhere, I felt a fiery tingling all over my body.

This wasn't a simple feeling of excitement or a burst of random energy. This unknown presence invaded my space with a power I had never felt. It was as if I was the bull's eye on whom all of heaven was focused. My body grew hot from the inside out, and electric-like tingles pulsated from my head to my toes. It felt like I was being cooked inside an oven. Beads of sweat formed on my forehead, and tears formed in my eyes. It felt like my finger had been placed in a light socket, but it was a strangely intense and pleasant electrocution.

As the fire continued, with my heart as its burning embers, some tears began to make their way down my red cheeks. My mind started spinning as I lifted my hands from their resting position on my legs and turned my palms upward. I stared at them, curious to know if any of this was visible to my natural eyes. I didn't have a clear explanation of what was happening, except that, in some way, this might be God manifesting Himself to me.

It lasted thirty seconds. Everything around me was as normal as could be. I know because I tried my best to look in every direction without giving away what was happening. My world was interrupted by a powerful and invisible reality much greater than mine.

I began an internal conversation with myself, "What is this?" As wild and uncontrollable as it was, it felt safe. It was unpredictable, yet it came with warmth and a ferocious comfort. I liked it. I felt like I was the bottom of the funnel into which God was pouring Himself. As the power of this force wore off, I thought, "Did I ask for this? Was this happening to anyone around me?" These questions ricocheted through my head like bullets gone astray. The people around me appeared perfectly normal, intent on obeying all the rules. "Was this other-worldly experience happening to any of them?"

I assure you that I was the least likely candidate for this type of experience with God. If the people who knew me were voting on whom this should happen, I doubt I would have made anyone's list. All the while, I tried hard not to let anyone know that anything out of the norm was taking place during this episode.

This supernatural phenomenon was far outside my grid for life, and God certainly hadn't asked my permission to do this, whatever "this" even was. My conclusion at the time was that this, in some way, was probably God, although I didn't dare talk to anyone about it. Leading up to this, I may or may not have prayed some sort of prayer like, "God, if you're real, let me know."

I can now see that this supernatural infusion of God's Spirit shifted my vision, making me much more sensitive to the world around me. I didn't have enough spiritual maturity to recognize this then, but this encounter birthed something powerful within me.

This violent but peaceful, disrupting but comforting, and wild but safe encounter with God didn't stop there. I had a handful or more of these short and intensely wonderful meetings as they bore a resemblance to the first. I never knew when this unknown and adventurous heavenly invasion was coming, nor did I know what was happening, but it continued.

It happened while sitting distant and blurry-minded in those uncomfortable Mormon Church pews. It happened at home. It even occurred out with friends.

With these encounters fresh on my mind and spirit, life began to take a turn, and it did so quickly.

CHAPTER 3
So It Begins

RR

WHAT DOES A lost and confused teenager do after a series of wild encounters with God? I didn't feel comfortable talking to anyone about it. I didn't think anyone would believe me, so I tried to process these unexplainable moments with God by myself. That was a problem because I didn't have the answers or even know the right questions to ask. With these questions in mind, a whole new world opened up to me.

In today's world, there is a lot of information educating people, especially young people, about the dangers of drug and alcohol use. Back then, my understanding of drugs and alcohol was, "Don't do it." In my real world, though, I was getting a crash course surrounding the fact that drugs and accessibility far outweighed the amount of education and support to help youth steer clear of them.

Taking it a step further, painkillers were not even talked about at this time. I had never heard of "pain pills" up until this point. This was my framework for life when the enemy began pulling my soul down the dark path of addiction.

After my series of encounters with God, the enemy knew he had to do something. His next move was sending the grim reaper "opiates" into my life.

I was fourteen years old, and the habits of smoking weed and drinking were already established in my young life. I can now say I didn't have a clue what I was getting myself into. Deep down, I knew what I was doing was wrong, but that in and of itself did not stop me from hopping on the deadly roller coaster of a party lifestyle. I just wanted to fit in, have fun, and escape.

I was a kid living in Utah, of all places. The year was 1996, and it was the infancy of Big Pharma unleashing hell on America in the form of prescribed opiates. Until 1996, the medical community measured our health using four vital signs: body temperature, pulse rate, respiration rate, and blood pressure. In 1996, "pain" was unofficially added to the vital sign list, and in 2001, "The Joint Commission" officially added pain as the 5th vital sign.

The problem with adding pain as a vital sign is that doctors cannot measure our pain because such a measurement is based solely on what we tell our doctors and what we tell our doctors they typically go with. So, someone can go to their doctor and tell them that they are experiencing level ten pain, and seeing that pain is considered a vital sign, painkillers are prescribed.

Amid this shift in medical thinking and services, I was a young teenager already wading into the river of addiction. Coming off these God moments with the demon of addiction tightening its grip on me, I was in a battle for my soul, and I didn't even know it. Then, one night, the door opened, and, unknowing to me, a guest entered my life that would speed up my destruction.

One night, at the age of fourteen, I had an excruciating toothache. On this night, our dentist kindly agreed to meet me at his office. He quickly diagnosed that I needed a root canal. The next day was the championship game of our freshman football season. Growing up, I was one of the best players on local and school baseball and football teams. I was excited for the next day and the chance to help my team become champions.

But the intensity of this pain had me writhing. Shortly thereafter, I was in the dentist's chair, and he was drilling into my tooth. He could not perform the root canal at that time, but drilling into my infected tooth allowed the pus to drain and the hideous pressure I felt to be somewhat relieved. He gave me a prescription for an antibiotic, but the tooth needed to continue draining until he could perform the root canal that coming Monday.

A drilled-out tooth, not filled in, equals pain. You take a breath, and the air hits the

exposed nerves. He also prescribed a bottle of painkillers (Vicodin) as a departing gift to minimize my pain. I was unaware of what Vicodin did, what it was, what it was for, or how it made me feel. It may as well have been Tylenol for all I was concerned.

Again, this was before the "opioid epidemic," if you can even imagine such a time in America. This was before an average of over 290 people dying daily due to drug overdoses in our nation. I had no idea what was coming. Pain blinded me as I walked through the doors and into the world of pills. It started with a bottle with my name on it saying, "Take 1-2 every 4-6 hrs. as needed for pain."

After leaving the late-night dental procedure, we stopped to fill the prescriptions, and my dad and I headed home. I was given two high-powered painkillers and went to sleep. I don't recall the immediate euphoria being birthed within me as I went to bed that night. After all, I wasn't expecting it. I didn't know what to expect.

The next day, however, my pain was real and raw as the big game quickly approached. Far be it from me to miss the biggest game of the season. I had worked too hard with my fellow teammates to miss this. With an intense toothache and a trusted doctor granting the magic fix in the form of painkillers, my parents lovingly gave me two Vicodin every six hours, just as prescribed.

One thing researchers did come to understand as they studied the process of turning opium into different forms of drugs—as it makes its way through pharmaceutical labs or street labs—is that Vicodin isn't the same thing as pure heroin. However, its effects on the mind and body are the same. Its potency is dependent upon how much processing the deadly morphine molecule has gone through from its beginnings in the opium fields of Afghanistan (the supplier of 80% of the world's opium) until the time it reaches your bloodstream. Depending on the type of pill someone is prescribed, some pills are more potent than pure heroin. For instance, fentanyl is fifty times more potent than pure heroin.

On the day of the championship game, the only thing that would have kept me from playing in that game would have been two broken legs. Even taking the pills before the game, I was still in pain, but I suited up and played. At one point, I remember coming out of the game and collapsing to the ground on the sideline. My helmet was still on as I lay there, geared up from head to toe as a seemingly fit and active teenager. Yet I lay writhing on the ground, grasping my face mask and crying as tears streamed down my face from the throbbing pain created less than 24 hours earlier by a drilled-out tooth and a raw, exposed nerve.

I still recall today, in vivid memory, looking up at a few grown men helplessly looking down at me, my father included, and realizing that none of them knew what to do to fix my situation. Something in me must have shifted as I lay there; maybe it was those deadly Vicodin candies filling more of my bloodstream with their charming effects, or maybe it was a deep and passionate desire to compete on that grand stage in that season. Whatever the reason, I went back into the game and played my heart out, although we ended up losing.

And the result of all this? Unbeknownst to me, the beginning of my chemical romance with opiates had begun. Life deals all of us pain, whether physical or emotional, at times. It's how we deal with pain that dictates the following sequences in our lives.

During its initial trial run, the floating on-air euphoria of Vicodin's effects didn't fully seduce me. After my parents gave them to me as prescribed and the pain vanished, that bottle of pharmaceutical candy found its place in the family medicine cabinet. But my addictive habits were deepening their roots within me, and without even knowing what was taking place, that silent bottle began to speak to me from the closed doors of the kitchen medicine cabinet.

In the coming weeks and months, I heard more conversations among friends about the enjoyable high that pain pills brought. Those whispers became normal chatter in the halls of my high school as the perfect storm that had rested on the horizon of my life made its way into the present. All while that half-full bottle of Vicodin lay dormant but deadly in our middle-class medicine cabinet.

That counterfeit voice of peace and joy kept calling me until, one night, I decided to obey its dark directive. I plotted the whole event in my mind before acting it out. I got a 40-ounce bottle of beer and grabbed two Vicodin. I swallowed those two tickets to paradise down with 40 ounces of alcohol, and off I went with my sister and some friends to shoot pool.

As the depths of deceit seduced me, I began to believe I was mature beyond my years—simply because of the ever-growing amounts of marijuana and alcohol I consumed. Few things manipulate and warp one's perspective of real life more than addiction does.

I remember pulling into the pool hall, but with the way the alcohol and painkillers were mixing in my bloodstream, I felt like I had not only arrived at the pool hall...I was convinced I had arrived in life. All my troubles vanished in the wind as euphoria took root within my entire being, and that critical internal chitter chatter went silent.

My eyes drooped with sedated satisfaction, as did my body language. My motor skills stumbled into what I thought was the perfect mode of operation. Suddenly, I was convinced there was nothing I couldn't do...of course, I would do it all tomorrow. For now, I would enjoy my escape to pill paradise.

Chaotically content with circling the pool table, I scanned the room in hopes of, well... I hadn't figured that part out yet. The pool stick was as light as a pencil in my hand, and it didn't matter if I made every shot or missed every shot. My inner world had found the remedy to the internal disease that had been growing within me. It was a counterfeit peace at best, as a pharmaceutical band-aid became duct tape over the internal pain, when spiritual surgery was what was truly needed.

While I felt light as a feather and nimble all at the same time, I was also heavy and sluggish. I felt confident and secure, but in reality, I was hiding from the world and completely afraid of the future. It felt like I'd put on an internal Snuggie and was floating through a hazy movie reel with little old me as the main character.

I felt as though I had opened the door of my soul and let someone else hop in the driver's seat. I was convinced that this initial ride with the morphine molecule coursing through my veins, purely for the sake of euphoria, was the way it would always be. It was a ride I never wanted to end.

What I didn't know was that this love affair and sense of false perfection would eventually flee. Not only did it flee, but it left a miserable replacement. The high wore off, and the low took its place. I went on an ascent for a few hours like I was waltzing in wonderland to a sharp descent and shifty sickness for the remainder of the night. I went from pure confidence and comfort to annoyance and uncertainty. It was a nasty emotional roller coaster of insanity.

As the night ended, and the morphine-molecule-induced movie I thought I was starring in came to its close, we made our way home. What I didn't know was that what was taking place in my body was the birthing of a dependency, both physiologically and psychologically.

I was clueless that what I had experienced wasn't just a physical high. It was also an emotional high that silences the voice of pain for a brief moment, only for the voice of pain to increase when the euphoria drifts away. I certainly didn't know, as I know now, what was taking place in my body when the Vicodin made its way into my bloodstream. If we look under the hood, here's what's going on. Our body's neurons are covered in proteins called "opioid receptors." Our body's natural opioid receptors produce a natural painkiller when pain is introduced to our body. These natural painkillers are called Endorphins.

When Endorphins are released, they slow down our body's ability to send pain signals to the brain. What painkillers do is they attach to our natural opioid receptors. Once attached, they cause our body to unnaturally produce and flood our bloodstream with a chemical that our body naturally produces called Dopamine. Dopamine plays a big part in the human body's ability to feel pleasure. This natural pleasure chemical is produced in us through eating the right foods, getting enough exercise and sleep, and prayer and meditation. And it can also be boosted through certain health supplements.

Dopamine is not the problem; our body naturally produces it. The problem comes when we take opiates, which send our body into overdrive and drain our natural dopamine reserves, hijacking the needed healing process with an addictive reprieve. When those reserves are drained, the body becomes dependent on the artificial feelings created by certain painkillers, and addiction sinks its hooks into our souls.

I knew nothing of this at the time. At the time, I also didn't know that opiates don't just kill physical pain; they also kill emotional pain. For a moment, that is. Emotional pain was ever-present within me, but painkillers instantly changed that. And it didn't just change it; it instantaneously changed my feeling of pain to a feeling of pleasure.

With no idea how to face this pain or life in general, I convinced myself I needed more opiates to "feel good."

CHAPTER 4
The High-Speed Chase

RR

I DON'T KNOW WHY some teenagers try smoking weed and don't like it, and some love it and then can't satisfy the insatiable craving that kicks in. The same goes for drinking, popping pills, and the list goes on and on. Why does everyone react differently internally and externally?

Once I found something that would momentarily silence the internal noise within me resting at the decimal level of a high school marching band, I only wanted more. This unquenchable thirst for drugs and alcohol overtook my life before I realized what was happening, and with addiction comes consequences.

It was like an invisible bartender was looming in the shadows of my life and listening to my every word. I would complain about being in pain, and later that day, I would cross paths with pain pills. I would talk about being bored, wanting to have fun, and receiving an invitation to get drunk. As I spoke, this demonic bartender listened and simultaneously concocted chaotic cocktails that aimed to bring a rapturous respite to the present situation. However, with that came long-term pain and confusion. As the normal and emotional ups and downs of being a teenager continued, I found myself being offered the short-term solution to my issues in the form of an ever-increasing amount of pills, marijuana, and alcohol. I willingly accepted the suggested sedation this unseen bartender constantly prepared for me. My life was a ticking time bomb, a recipe for disaster, and I was blind to the fact that my illogical thinking made me the main ingredient and catalyst in this toxic turn of events.

Even when a therapeutic outlet occasionally presented itself, I didn't want to process any of it. I didn't know what was wrong with me. I hadn't experienced any trauma until that point, but an internal pain was certainly present. All the while, I had convinced myself I didn't need help.

I was in my sophomore year of high school. I had already been in trouble with the law for fighting. I had been in trouble at school for drugs, and I was the cause of more than a few problems within my family. By age fifteen, smoking weed and drinking were almost daily habits, and I took pills as often as possible. Sadly, more and more kids are leaning towards drugs as their outlet. The National Center for Drug Abuse Statistics states that half of teenagers have misused drugs.

This whirlwind of addiction reached its first chaotic climax in my life one day early in my sophomore year of high school. The fact about addiction is this—it always progresses. It's progressive in nature because our body develops a tolerance, and as that tolerance grows, the internal chaos and pain increase. As the pain increases and our tolerance increases, more and more drugs are needed to try and reclaim the euphoric feeling that a drug user once felt.

This next scene in my life movie climbed to a new level of insanity. I was a "good kid" raised in a good family. I lived in a good neighborhood, and I had emerging talents. My story is no different than hundreds that I've heard over the years. But one thing is for sure: I was unaware that there is a spiritual enemy that is out to "kill, steal, and destroy" the lives of anyone he can. I understand this now. I had been sucked into the vortex of the enemy's world, and he was hell-bent on destroying me.

My parents, older sister, and my younger brother had gone to England for ten days. My aunt was staying to supervise us. This family trip left a window of time for me to do what I wanted without consequence—or so I thought. On this day, there was no escaping the madness that had overtaken my life. I was roughly a year or more past the God encounters I previously described and well over a year into the world of addiction. After deciding we'd had enough of school for the day, my friends and I thought it would be a good idea to start drinking around noon. So, we left at lunch and began stealing alcohol from the stores in the area. This wasn't the first time we had used the stores throughout the city as our own open bar.

The stealing and drinking continued all day with no remorse and no notion of where the day was taking us. Coincidentally, another one of my friends (we will call him Dave) parents were out of town during this same time. Dave had a car, which none of the rest of us had. So, with Dave as our chauffeur, the city as our drunken playground, and Dave's parents' house as our base of operations, the stage was set for a dramatic ending as our insanity carried on until well past midnight.

As our mental faculties became soaked deeper and deeper in inebriation, our judgment became increasingly reckless—even though we didn't think so. I knew what I was doing was problematic. But impaired and confused thinking made me incapable of seeing what was happening to me, let alone let me see the big picture of where I was heading and the violent spiritual vortex into which I had been sucked.

What most people don't acknowledge, let alone realize, is that alcohol is a drug. The Oxford Dictionary defines a drug as "a medicine or other substance which has a physiological effect when ingested or otherwise introduced into the body." Alcohol is, without question, a drug.

Void of much maturity to begin with and being hours into a wild binge, there was no good way that this night was going to end. At the least, I could have gone to sleep to wake up with a nasty hangover. That would have been a fairytale ending compared to what played out.

It was past midnight, and Craig (who we will call this friend) and I decided we should make one more run for alcohol. Our logic was that we would need some for the next day if the fun were to continue. So, the final ascent to our climatic chaos was set in motion.

The first thing we needed was a vehicle, so we stole the keys from a sleeping friend's pocket (we will call this friend Cory), who had joined us in our escapades. These keys just happened to be the keys to his mother's minivan, and we thought, why not? We'll be back in ten minutes. Keys in hand, we set off to make one last theft of alcohol, fully intending to be back in time to get some rest before another day of drinking.

We thought it would be a good idea to circle back to the same grocery store we stole alcohol from twice that day. We made our way down the dark and vacant streets of Utah County's middle-class suburbia toward the store we had singled out. Craig was in the driver's seat.

We approached our destination, and Craig pulled into the grocery store parking lot. The lights shone out from the storefront windows like spotlights aimed right at us. Those spotlights seemed to pulsate on us as he slammed the minivan into park and told me to hop into the driver's seat. Apparently, I was driving us out of there, and I was told to be ready to do it with gusto.

I readily complied, oblivious to the fact that the stage was now set for a nightmarish scene straight out of a horrible action movie. Craig ran inside to grab our next day's supply of beer, expecting to skate out of there for the third time that day with little or no hassle.

One of the many issues in play at that moment was one that neither Craig nor I had considered. I had never driven a car. I was utterly clueless as to how to operate a motor vehicle. Take that interesting puzzle piece and add to it the fact that my blood was fueled by hours and hours of alcohol consumption, and now a healthy shot of adrenaline, and the stage was set for the next scene in this disastrous movie.

Moments later, Craig came running out of the store with four cases of beer. He ran as fast as he awkwardly could with a case of beer under each arm and one in each hand. He opened the sliding door and threw our next day's beer supply into the minivan. He yanked open the front passenger side door and launched into the seat. "Step on the gas!" he yelled. And with that commenced my first-ever driving experience.

I slammed the gas pedal down as a store employee came out after us, yelling and demanding we stop. As the minivan picked up speed out of the parking lot, I at least proved I knew which pedal was the gas and which was the brake. We sped off, and I swerved my way out of the large parking lot right across the main street of the city. Pulling into the four-lane street, I bounced over the concrete median strip. However, as quickly as I thought we were home free, a last hurdle presented itself.

A police cruiser just happened to be pulling out of the police station, which was kitty-corner to the grocery store we had just stolen alcohol from for the third time that day.

He flipped on his lights, made a U-Turn, and my first driving experience got a little more interesting. This cocktail of alcohol, panic, emotions, and adrenaline threw me into survival mode. I floored the gas pedal with the intention of making my way towards some back streets and neighborhoods with which I was more familiar.

Never "in my right mind" would I have driven a car on the roads without ever practicing first, let alone get in a drunken high-speed chase in these suburban neighborhoods. However, it was far too late to stop and implement any logic.

As I sped down the street in a fierce yet dreamlike state of chaos, I made another sharp right turn with glaring lights and a haunting siren screaming behind us. I was now speeding down residential streets right past our high school from where we had skipped out earlier that day. A few blocks down that road, Craig screamed at me to stop the car. Without thinking, I slammed on the brakes, and he jumped out and began sprinting off through a park.

My split-second assessment of his actions made some sort of sense to me. I drove another hundred feet or so and did the exact same thing. I hit the brakes and jumped out of the car. Without putting it in park, I ran in the opposite direction as fast as possible.

The minivan rolled into a streetlight. In my drunken state of mind, I was determined that taking my shirt off would somehow help me elude the authorities.

Alcohol-filled sweat began to seep out of my pores as I listened to the distant yelling of police officers and their indistinct radio chatter. I could see flashlights scanning narrow gaps between houses. More squad cars arrived on the scene, as my heart rate quickened.

As crazy and impossible as it seemed, I somehow managed to elude the authorities as I hopped fences into other neighborhoods in the pandemonium of those moments. It was an hour of frantically deserting the scene until I was sure I had made my escape. By this time, I was shirtless, sweaty, exhausted, and slowly gaining back a slight sense of sobriety. The adrenaline rush I experienced most likely brought a small sense of clarity to my mind. I recall thinking once or twice about Craig, hoping he, too, had escaped the ruckus.

Blurred as my thinking was, I suddenly recognized the neighborhood I was in and remembered a friend who lived close by (we will call him Henry). I somehow found my way to Henry's house, all the while ducking in the shadows and creeping through backyards. Once I arrived at my go-to destination, I checked both cars in the carport of his house, and one of them was open. Crawling into the backseat of the SUV, I luckily found a blanket in the car. Curling into a fetal position on the backseat, I pulled the blanket around my sweat-soaked body and passed out.

Sunlight snuck up on me in the backseat of my makeshift, uncomfortable but desperately needed bed. I awoke blurry-brained, but this was directly followed by another surge of adrenaline as movie reels of the prior night suddenly flashed through my mind.

I quickly exited the SUV with a sweat-soaked blanket wrapped around me. I thought it would be a good idea to knock on Henry's front door around seven a.m. on a weekday morning. Henry's mother answered to see me shirtless with her blanket as my covering, politely asking for her son.

She gave me a very peculiar look as she called for Henry. When he came to the door, he took one look at me and hurried me into the basement to his room. His mother soon followed, knocking on the door, asking what was going on and why her car smelled like sweat. The evidence was stacked against me. Somehow, Henry smoothed the situation over, and I showered and put on some fresh clothes.

As I sat in Henry's room, head still spinning from the night before, I explained the previous night's events as best I could. I sat on his bed, pondering my next move, knowing that I would eventually have to face the music. After weighing my options, with only a tiny portion of my thinking ability being operative, I figured that heading back to school was the best option. Seeing how he only lived a couple of blocks from the high school, we began to make the trek back to reality.

As I walked across the fields behind our school, where I played football and baseball, my heartbeat picked up speed. "What am I walking into?" I asked myself. Wishing I would wake up from a bad dream, I entered the school through the back doors, hoping I was invisible. I quickly realized I wasn't as I entered the main hangout area of the school, and some friends approached me to inform me that the police had been to the school looking for me and Craig.

Moments later, Craig appeared in the commons area as well. We looked at each other without words, confounded by what we should do next. Without time to recall the entirety and insanity of the previous night, after a quick conversation, we decided to turn ourselves into the same police station that we had zoomed past during the high-speed chase the night prior. Dave said he would drive us, and off we went with a bewildered look to face the law.

The five-minute drive felt like ten seconds as we tried to get our story straight before lying to the police. We arrived and slowly walked to the front door, expecting the worst while somehow knowing that this was the smartest play we had. "We're here to turn ourselves in for a crime we committed last night," I told the older lady behind the glass at the front desk. Looking perplexed, she replied, "Okay, just wait here, please." Moments later, a plainclothes officer opened the door and escorted us to the back rooms of the old musty police station.

They split Craig and me up and gathered our stories. The cop was very calm and, shockingly, understanding about the whole thing. After getting my story, he wrote me a citation for fleeing the scene, didn't even call my parents, and allowed me to leave. Once rendezvoused with Craig in the parking lot, he explained a similar story. To our chagrin, we received a slap on the wrist for our reckless and dangerous behavior.

My response to this? I got in a fight later the same day and was hauled off to a youth detention center until my parents returned home from overseas. You would think that these events would have scared me straight. Tragically, even with all the evidence of my life spiraling out of control, it was just the beginning.

CHAPTER 5
The Loony Bin

RR

EVEN AFTER MY night of high-speed destruction, I still thought I could manage the beast of addiction. My parents disciplined me and tried to get me some help, but I was very resistant to any help offered. The audacity of someone suggesting I needed help was offensive to my mind because I was riding high, literally.

My journey through high school was a wild ride. How I graduated is still beyond me. My high school days were filled with drugs, alcohol, fights, and all the while being a regionally recognized athlete. On more than one occasion, faculty members looked the other way as I got in fights, cheated on schoolwork, and possibly missed more school than I attended. Being the drug addict and alcoholic I was, I pushed the limits on these boundaries.

By the time I was sixteen, I knew what I was doing was wrong and taking me nowhere, but my hunger to numb the pain I felt within was stronger than my desire to change. I had no respect for life. I didn't even understand what respect for life meant. I thought what I was doing was no one else's business, and it only affected me. I thought I would be fine if everyone would leave me alone and let me live my life.

The truth is, if my family would have done that, I would have certainly died.

I didn't recognize that I was blind to reality. I was blind to anything except my desire for more drugs and alcohol. They weren't just crutches by this point in time; they were my lifeline.

My God encounters were a distant, yet not completely forgotten, moment in life. I would pray at times during this craziness, but only when I needed to be bailed out of consequences because of the poor choices I had made.

It didn't help that an avalanche of painkillers was being unleashed on America, and my friends and I were getting in on this euphoric deadliness on the ground floor. Most days, my friends and I fed our addiction by simply emptying any and all medicine cabinets into which we could get our hands on. Seeing how most people were still unaware of the dangers of pain pills, we quickly found the average medicine cabinet had some sort of pain pills in it. This made accessing pills pretty easy.

I had tunnel vision, and by this time, I was doing whatever I had to do to stay numb. An average day in the hallways of Orem High School consisted of walking from class to class—when I attended—and feeling like I was floating in euphoria. Followed by a physical crash and feeling sick hours later when the unnaturally manufactured dopamine wore off.

The night of my graduation in 2000, I thought I had reached a new level of addictive composure. I was so high on a cocktail of painkillers and anti-anxiety medications that I couldn't even feel the principal's hand when I shook it as he handed me my diploma.

A false sense of freedom was birthed as graduation from high school only clamped the shackles of addiction down even tighter. I had created in my mind an expectation of what life would be like after high school as responsibilities shifted to the rear-view mirror. I had convinced myself that I would be free to have some real fun once high school was done! The problem was that my definition of "real fun" was, in reality, like playing Russian Roulette daily.

I managed to get my own apartment the summer after graduating, and it quickly became the party spot. It was round-the-clock insanity.

I'm not sure how I kept my job as a busboy at a local restaurant, but somehow, I did.

In this season of my life, the reality of addiction got darker and darker as death entered the equation. The demon of addiction began taking the lives of my friends and acquaintances as early as high school. There were overdoses, suicides, freak accidents, car accidents, and so on. Each death in some way involved drugs and alcohol, and after high school, that list quickly grew.

The frequency with which friends died added an acute awareness of how lethal this lifestyle was, but it somehow did not resonate with me. My friends came and went like new clothing styles and began passing away nearly as fast. My methodical mixture of drugs, by choice, was a scary one. I was religiously drinking and mixing a variety of pills. This chaotic cocktail of suicidal substances has ended the lives of more beautiful souls than I care to remember.

The normal mind's logical response to this craziness is, "Okay, good run. Maybe it's time to try something different here?" However, the mind steeped in addiction, and its death grip says, "Man, you need to find a way to manage this so it stops getting so out of control." Yet the more I tried to manage it, the more concentrated and lethal my sinful sickness became. It was as if a dark, unseen spiritual entity was slowly feeding my mind lies, working overtime to convince me that everything was fine in my life. I thought I was enjoying all that life had to offer, but little did I know I was on a death march to an early grave.

During those dark days in my first summer fresh out of high school, another wake-up call came my way. One of my dear sisters, the one I am closest with to this day, was pregnant and due any day to give birth to her first child. This, of course, didn't stop me from living my normal out-of-control lifestyle. My reality was entirely self-centered and didn't leave any room for taking other people and their circumstances into consideration.

The special night came for her to deliver her first child and my parent's first grandchild. I had expressed an interest in being there, so my mom called and told me she was coming to pick me up to go to the hospital so we could all experience this wonderful moment together. I should have said no, but I was horribly drunk and tried to play it cool over the phone. She arrived, and before she could ascertain my mental state, I was in the car, and we were off to the hospital.

I was mumbling in broken sentences about not wanting to live anymore and threatening to jump out of the car. This night was ordained to be a celebration of life, and my idea of celebrating life had taken me to the brink of wanting to end mine.

My consciousness was skipping in and out of an alcohol-induced blackout. My mother, being the amazing mom that she is, was concerned for me. Upon arrival at the hospital, she mentioned my behavior to the security guards, desperate to get me help.

The next thing I recall was being trapped in a tiny room with two security guards putting me in handcuffs. While they were trying to figure out what to do with the situation, I told them, "I'll make you two a deal. You take these handcuffs off, and if I can knock you two out, I get to leave. If you two can take me out, then I stay."

The result?

I found myself a resident in the hospital's mental health resort -- I guess some people call it the "psych ward." As the alcohol wore off and I put on the gown I was required to wear as I spent the weekend in what many people call the loony bin, reality began to hit me. Sadly, that reality was not enough to make me want to change...yet.

My experience grew even more bizarre as my new roommate initiated a conversation on my first night there. He began by explaining his need to hoard an entire drawer of newspapers. Then he showed me the scars on his arms, scars he had clawed with his fingernails because he was determined to dig the people living inside of him out and into freedom.

Again, you would think this wake-up call would do just that: wake me up. Especially because the psych ward doctor had left for the day and wouldn't see patients again until Monday morning, and it was a Friday night. I had a long weekend ahead of me. I had time to think. I had time to reflect. I did some praying but mainly watched the clock in anticipation of Monday morning.

It is interesting that I was, by now, in the habit of talking to God as soon as trouble hit. Handcuffs and loss of freedom always boosted my prayer life, and I came from a home where prayer was a consistent part of our daily life. I would think back on the wild experiences that landed me in trouble and wonder what prayer was exactly. I would wonder who or what was God. Who is Jesus, anyway?

Something was imparted into my soul in those stiff church pews when God invaded my life without my permission. That "something" was this: I knew God was the answer. Talking with God in my mind, or at least talking about God and oftentimes begging Him for things wasn't abnormal to me. I knew deep down that only a relationship with God would set me free. But I had no idea what that looked like. Even if I did, I wasn't ready to do it. I had too many questions for God and too few answers coming my way. God was answering me, but my drug and alcohol-soaked mind and the demons around me blocked them.

Even that long weekend filled with bizarre conversations with people who had tragic, legitimate mental health issues wasn't enough for me to throw up my arms in surrender. In a very real way, God was showing me what my future would look like if I continued down this path. My response? I simply bulldozed through God's attempts to help me as He regularly placed red lights, blockades, and checkpoints in my path.

Monday morning came, and I was called to the doctor's office still dressed in my goofy gown. He told me what I already knew. He explained that I didn't qualify to be held at the mental health resort under mental health guidelines and state law but that I did need help. It was nothing I didn't already know.

So, what was the first thing I did when I got home on that bright, beautiful Monday morning? I finished the alcohol I didn't have the opportunity to finish on Friday night.

CHAPTER 6
Flirting With Death

RR

IN THE WORDS of Ron Burgundy from the movie "Anchorman, "That escalated quickly." I went from a normal, annoyed teenager to a suicidal, raging alcoholic and drug addict in a matter of a few years.

In our present recovery cultures, I believe one of the problems that stunt many recoveries is the lack of commitment to a vision for their future. George Washington Carver said it perfectly when he said, *"Where there is no vision, there is no hope."* What makes Carver's observation so powerful is that he was born into slavery in 1864, kidnapped as an infant and orphaned, grew up sickly, and yet still went on to achieve more than most could ever dream of accomplishing.

Carver faced outrageous adversity and persecution but walked with God through it all. In a letter to Isabelle Coleman in 1931, he explained, "I was just a mere boy when [I] converted, hardly ten years old. There isn't much of a story to it. God just came into my heart one afternoon while I was alone in the 'loft' of our big barn while I was shelling corn to carry to the mill to be ground into meal." That encounter with God was central to the life of the visionary man who served as the first principal of The Tuskegee Institute and the first president of Tuskegee University.

Along with his lengthy resume of academic achievements, Carver is renowned for his extraordinary achievements in agricultural science. A devout man of faith, Carver found over 300 beneficial uses from the peanut. History.com details, "In all, he developed more than 300 food, industrial, and commercial products from peanuts, including milk, Worcestershire sauce, punches, cooking oils and salad oils, paper, cosmetics, soaps, and wood stains. He also experimented with peanut-based medicines, such as antiseptics, laxatives, and goiter medications."

Throughout his life, Carver gave credit to God for all his successes. As documented by Carver's early biographer Rackham Holt – whose book Carver reviewed before his death – the Tuskegee scientist long mused over grand scientific problems and took his questions to God in prayer. The Missouri Baptist Convention journal, The Pathway, describes that Carver "had a little story," as Holt wrote, "in which he related his experience: "I asked the Great Creator what the universe was made for. 'Ask for something more in keeping with that little mind of yours,' He replied. 'What was man made for?' 'Little man, you still want to know too much. Cut down the extent of your request and improve the intent.'"

After this conversation, Carver narrowed his pursuit of knowledge down to a peanut. He took a handful of peanuts to the lab, and the rest is history. If Carver could rely on God and bring forth such remarkable achievements under challenging circumstances and in an environment as oppressive as slavery and racism, what can God, a vision, and a hopeful shift in perspective do for a suffering addict or alcoholic?

Time and time again, I've witnessed people try and step into recovery and fall into the trap of thinking that if they can stop drinking and using drugs, everything will magically fall into place. I tried this multiple times myself, only to fall back into unhealthy patterns time and time again. This happens because years and years of warped thinking burrow deep roots into the psyche, and they will not disappear with a snap of the fingers. Perilous patterns of thought ensnare themselves spiritually and physiologically in the mind and the heart of an addict.

Addressing these issues is essential to establishing a hope-filled vision for the future. It is a key ingredient in any recipe for recovery.

Jesus talked about a faith the size of a "mustard seed." Carver used a peanut. When it comes to the recovery process, a particle of faith mixed with action, a vision, and hope for the future contains enough power to transform a life beyond recognition.

On more than one occasion, I would manage some sobriety from drugs and alcohol by simply "white-knuckling it," as it is often called. I'd hang on for dear life and sometimes collect a few days, sometimes a few weeks, and there was the rare occasion where a month or two of sobriety would surface. But those times were filled with uncertainty, a bottomless pit of shame, unending guilt, gut-wrenching regret, and emotional and mental exhaustion because I had not gotten to the root of the problem. I had not adopted basic, essential life skills that would help me stay free from addiction. Consequently, I inevitably returned to what I knew, escaping reality through self-medicating.

After high school graduation and a long summer that went by in the blink of a blurry eye, I somehow lived through the insanity in that horrifying hub of an apartment. At the end of that run, I had nothing. I had no vision for the future and no desire to better myself. All I had done was stretch the boundary lines of chaos and dig the hole deeper. So, with my head hanging low and nowhere else to go, I begged my parents to let me come back and live in their home. But just before the end of that addictive vortex, I recall one night in that apartment when the spirit of death nearly guided me into slow-motion suicide.

The consistent news of friends' lives ending at the hands of the demon of addiction affected me in ways I didn't perceive at the time. The fear of my life ending abruptly was a growing internal conversation, but no life-giving solutions came from dialoguing with myself. One night, as another cocktail of pills entangled themselves in my bloodstream and numbing euphoria grew within me, life flashed before my eyes. There I was, sitting on my couch with a couple of girls, and it was as if someone slowed the frames per second in a movie as my motor skills went into slow motion. I began to feel the cadence of my pulse slow, and there was a thumping in my head akin to the energizer bunny running out of batteries.

Somehow, one sane thought made its way into the operating system of my mind. The thought was, "call the paramedics." I know now that this life-preserving thought was not my own, nor did I have the physical strength at the time to follow up on this counsel.

These years later, it is clear that God was helping me long before I ever desired to help myself. I called the paramedics from my cell phone and told them I would meet them outside, fearing the police would join them and bombard my apartment. I intentionally withheld my apartment number and made the parking lot the rendezvous spot.

My legs somehow made their way down a couple of flights of stairs like a scene out of "Fear and Loathing in Las Vegas." The ambulance pulled up, I causally hopped in the back, and they began checking me out. I was as honest as I wanted to be, and they gave me advice based on what I told them and how fast my heart was beating. Surprisingly, they told me I would be okay and should sleep it off. I cracked a heavy and despondent smile and exited the ambulance as slowly as I got in it. Nowadays, an immediate trip to the hospital would be protocol, but those days it was not.

I made my way back up what seemed like endless flights of stairs and into my dark den, wondering what had just happened. The two females I'd left behind were still there, unaware of my full history and relationship with drugs. They looked at me with perplexed faces and left. I sat alone, acutely aware of my heartbeat as I pondered my life.

And that was that. It was a weird night to add to my growing list of death-defying new norms. I somehow lived through that night and many nights like it. Unfortunately, many of my friends did not.

Returning to my parent's home at the end of that summer made me feel like baseball player Bill Buckner returning to Shea Stadium after the 1986 World Series. It was back to rules and curfews and what I perceived to be a loss of freedom, all the while doing the best I could to hide the reality of what my life had become.

It is interesting to look back and see how my addiction, just like that of so many other's addictions, kicked in and grew in proportion to the opioid epidemic. One number that has skyrocketed, alongside the saddening number of people who didn't make it out of addiction, is the staggering increase in the number of people who have taken their lives in the last twenty years. Of course, not everyone who tragically takes their life does so because of drug and alcohol abuse. Yet, sadly, it is often a factor.

Since 2000, the annual deaths in America due to drugs and alcohol has nearly doubled. Well over 200,000 people a year are dying from drugs and alcohol. Those numbers jump dramatically among people in their 20s and 30s.

My issues were self-inflicted—yet the truth is that some people's issues are not self-inflicted. Some people are thrust into the world of depression and addiction because the environments in which they reside and the practices they see all around them offer little or no chance to observe or choose a different path—a better path. This was not the case in my life.

This is likely one of the reasons my depression got so thick; no one was responsible for my madness but me. My addiction had reached a point where real fun or joy had evaporated. To be perfectly truthful, I felt like I was having fun at one point, but now it was pretty much nonexistent. My drinking and using were more maintenance to try and quiet the internal storm and silence terrifying thoughts of the challenges of trying to live a normal life.

By age nineteen, in continuous conversation with myself, I had convinced myself that the only way out was death. I had tried to find the exit door from the haunted house of addiction, but all to no avail. I had tried to manage it, only to drown in it. The darkness that followed me like a cloud over my head had me believing that suicide was the only way to get out of this pain and insanity. I had no vision—therefore, I had no hope.

The volume on the thought of ending my life had been increasing for years. Still, up until now, my life had not yet gotten to the hopeless point where I embraced the invitation to engage in a premeditated act that would result in my certain demise. It had now. I was done. Regret ate at me like a starving dog, shame screamed in my ear through a bullhorn, and hope had exited stage left years prior.

At nineteen years old, I decided that it was time to go. I was back living with my parents and stumbling through a halfhearted attempt at life as I plotted my exit plan.

In 2021, 48,183 people committed suicide in the United States (CDC.GOV), and over 700,000 people do so around the globe. If you add to that number over 200,000 deaths from drugs and alcohol, there are well over 250,000 people a year dying in the United States of America from suicide and overdoses. All those people who died had amazing destinies and callings on their lives. Every person struggling with addiction today has an amazing destiny and calling in their life. They need to know that no matter how bad it is or has been...there is a way out. God can transform anyone's life.

However, on this particularly dark day, I did not know this great truth. Therefore, I planned to gas myself to death, to let carbon monoxide slowly poison me into permanent sleep. I found a day after everyone else left for work or school when I would be the only one home during the morning. I pulled the family van into the garage for what I thought would be the final scene in my hopeless life.

The garage door closed like a stone rolling in front of a tomb. I closed all the windows in the family van and laid the seats down. It was a sick picture that paralleled my life to that point. I had closed my mind to the idea that I could find any real outside help and decided to end it all. Just like I had been doing all along with choices and actions in my life, I shut everything out and settled on poisoning myself to answer life's problems.

With the windows shut except for a slight crack in the rear window for the hose to pump the carbon monoxide into the van where my family and I had made so many memories—I turned the van on and laid down to sleep.

But God…

A ten-minute drive away, my sister sat in her home on the other side of town. This was the same sister my mom picked me up to go and be with on the night she gave birth to her first child. While sitting at home that morning, my sister later explained that she "just had a feeling that she should head to Mom and Dad's, for whatever reason." That impression would not leave her alone. She didn't know I was home and certainly didn't know why she was going, but she acted on that impression and went.

At the same time, as I lay inside the cushioned full-size van, inhaling hell, I grew increasingly tired. I wasn't thinking about how shockingly selfish taking my own life was. I was thinking about how desperately I wanted the madness to end. It was all about me and my pain.

God only knows how much longer it might have been before the final page of my earthly life was written. It couldn't have been much longer. Suddenly, the stone before the tomb was rolled away—and the garage door opened. I was shocked. I sat up as shame gripped me. There stood my sister.

Before the garage door opened, she frantically opened the van door and asked me what I was doing. I hopped out the other side of the van and quickly made my way inside and downstairs. I laid on the couch and pulled a huge blanket over my head, wishing all the while that my life would just end.

My sister called and informed my parents, and they immediately hurried home and tried to talk to me through the blanket. I would not reply, let alone give them answers to the questions they asked. They finally, cautiously, let me have my space as they periodically monitored me. The depth of darkness within me only turned up the volume on the shame and guilt I felt. My physical body was still alive, but my spirit and soul were six feet under.

CHAPTER 7
The Merry-Go-Round of Addiction

RR

I CAN LOOK BACK and say that even in the darkest times of my painful journey, God's fingerprints were all over the details of my life. Looking back now, I can say with conviction that He would speak to me in moments of frantic panic, and even when I wished for death, His absolute love would pierce through my darkness.

Even at times when I wanted to end my life there was, deep in the recesses of my frayed consciousness, a glimmer of hope and faith that one day, in the future, life would be better. And although that spark never entirely left me, I was often unable to recognize it or blatantly ignored it. Even as my life slowly got worse and fear tightened its grip on me, feelings of faith sometimes made their way into my mind and stimulated glimpses of God's love for me, of who I was and who I could become. Those fleeting windows often closed as fast as they opened, but the lovely, fresh, gentle breezes they provided were desperately needed.

I believe the small, simple seed of faith planted in my heart those years prior enabled me to hear God's whispers of love in the dark times. That sort of faith cannot be mustered up on its own. That mustard seed of trust did not originate with me. It was an act of grace on God's part. It's His gift to any of us that will receive it. Those fiery encounters with God's power and love years prior embedded a hope in my hollowed-out soul, and that hope was warring for my life even when walking with God was clearly still not a priority for me.

I have lived over fourteen years free from those dark and hellish days. One thing that I see with constant acuity is how deep individuals dig themselves into a "rock bottom" pit. I did it for years. I have often heard people talk about their "rock bottom" like it is some sort of badge of honor.

My motive for sharing my story is not to share how awesome I was at my destruction or how grand I am today because I live free. Anything but! My prayer and purpose is that my story of going from chaos to freedom will give voice to the unspoken internal chaos many addicts and alcoholics battle daily. My hope is that the steps I took and continue to take, and the changes I have made and will continue to make, will help others find a way out. That it will provide a roadmap of sorts to help guide others to freedom.

Have you ever observed the train wreck some people's lives have become and wondered, "Why don't they hit the brakes, jump off, and get on another train?" I'm confident that almost everyone who observed my past life would have said something along those lines, if not something worse. The problem with such thinking is that, while it might be true, it doesn't help the person caught in addiction get out of the spiritual prison in which they are locked.

To this day, it baffles me how many people have little or no under-standing of the reality of demons and their schemes, especially those who have faith in God or those who are in the church. It is baffling that they have no understanding that there are evil forces in the world and that Satan seeks every opportunity to deceive and destroy. You cannot effectively fight an enemy you know nothing about, let alone an enemy that some barely acknowledge exists. One of the most misunderstood aspects of drug and alcohol addiction is the alarming magnitude with which individuals allow spiritual darkness to come into their lives. I would have never done the things I did if I knew that doing so would invite demons to enter my life to torment me.

The fact that darkness drove me to live this life of insanity does not vindicate my actions. Only God can do that. Everyone is responsible for their choices to open those doors and allow the vicious vortex of spiritual imprisonment into their life. What is this vortex of spiritual torment like? In many ways, it can be compared to riding a merry-go-round, although a grotesque one. Have you ever ridden a merry-go-round?

My wife and I, and two children (at that time), lived in Ohio for just over two years, and while there, we would frequently take our sons to the Akron Zoo. We would wander the zoo and enjoy the exhibits, but the boys especially loved the merry-go-round. Waiting in line, we watched the people lined up ahead of us excitedly point out which animal they wanted to ride when their turn came. My boys did the same thing, except when it was their turn, they would go from animal to animal, changing their minds about which animal to ride.

Once they decided on their imaginary escort, the four of us would spin in circles as they laughed and enjoyed the adventurous make-believe world they had entered for a short time. But then the ride would stop. The ride always stops. And when it did, they strongly voiced their displeasure and resisted as we tried to herd them to the exit.

The joy of watching our children enter that imaginative, exciting jungle world was deeply entertaining and enjoyable for us as parents. Children have an incredibly beautiful, innocent zeal for life. Their imagination hasn't yet been shaped or sometimes ruined by disappointment and the craziness this world can produce.

Addiction parallels the merry-go-round experience—far more so than one may think. As a teenager, I just wanted to find joy in life. I wanted to find a world I could escape to and come alive in, and I wanted to believe that there was more to life than what my natural eyes could see. I know now that there is a world of joy, excitement, fulfillment, and wonder to be had. There is so much more to life than our natural eyes often observe – and it is beautiful. But alongside the beautiful realm that promotes life, there is a realm that promotes death.

As a teenager, I watched the "cool kids" partying with what seemed like no care in the world, and it looked appealing. It was as if I was standing in line for the merry-go-round, hoping for a chance to ride. In truth, I had no clue what I was waiting in line for.

When I finally got my chance to get on the merry-go-round of the partying lifestyle, I made my way around the platform with eyes of wonder, trying to decide which creature to climb on and ride. However, the merry-go-round of drugs and alcohol was nothing like the fun, cute, imaginative ride most merry-go-rounds provide. Little did I know I was entering into a macabre gyration whose treachery was accompanied by eerie and creepy circus music.

I soon found myself going in circles and circles. When the ride ended, I wanted to pick another creature and continue endlessly circling instead of exiting. And when you stay on the ride long enough, you come to believe the lie that there is no other choice available to you but to keep riding. Each and every time the ride stopped and the music ended, I could have exited the ride, but instead, I just picked another creature and continued going in circles.

The demonic grip of addiction convinces individuals that there is no way out. And as I sat on the hideous merry-go-round, the creatures that came with the ride would whisper promises of grandiose living in my ear— but only if I stayed on the ride. I would switch drugs, or switch girlfriends, or switch groups of friends. But I didn't get off the ride because I didn't know how to. I allowed the ever-circling motion to suck me in, numb me, deaden my senses, and act as a screwdriver, slowly twisting me into my grave.

A short stay in jail, or rehab, occasionally forced me off the chaotic circus ride. Yet, addicted to its evil allures, as soon as I had the choice, and I always had a choice, I climbed back on the creatures turned monsters, thinking it offered real freedom when, in fact, it was nothing more than a ghastly swiveling of ghoulishly malevolent ghosts who had succeeded at their task of ensnaring me.

Shortly after an ecstasy overdose, I willingly went to my first rehab in downtown Salt Lake City. It was an intense program, very structured and very confrontational. This program was not voluntary for most of the inhabitants as most were mandated to be there by the court. This was their last chance to escape further imprisonment and gain their freedom. Their actions forced them to choose to finish the program or serve their sentence.

There I was, a twenty-one-year-old with the emotional maturity of a thirteen-year-old, thrown into a mosh pit of tension and attempted recovery. Shockingly, I did pretty well in the program. I had been there for about four months and had reached level three of a four level program. How? Or better to ask, WHY? Simple, fear drove me.

Fear can be a wonderful motivator, but it is a terrible master. I wasn't obeying program rules in an attempt to genuinely overcome my addictions. Instead, I obeyed because I was terrified that these people would discover the extent of endless confusion and pain within me. Over time, my fellow rehabbers and the staff were getting too close, and I realized that they would soon demand that I begin to open up about the pain and sickness in my life. I was not ready or willing to do that.

As my fear and anxiety built up over four months, the thought of honestly speaking about my inner world in a group setting became too much to bear. So, one day, I walked out the front door, leaving all my stuff behind. I found a phone I could use at a store a few blocks from the house. My first call was to my mother. When I called and asked her to come and get me and let me move home, she begged me to return and finish the program. When I told her I wouldn't return, she said she would not come and get me, and I could not come home. I hung up and called my friends. They came and picked me up immediately.

What did I do? I jumped right back on the merry-go-round. I was smoking weed and high within an hour or two after leaving the rehab facility. In less than two days, I had renewed my disastrous relationship with alcohol. Within two weeks of riding in circles on that maniacal merry-go-round, I was back to guzzling liquor to drown out my pain and confusion, and another pinnacle of chaos was imminent.

One night, just a few weeks after walking out the front door of rehab, I decided on a night of heavy drinking. I went to a friend's house, where we quickly drank one bottle of Jack Daniels. I drank most of it.

I soon left his house to head to another party. Stumbling out of his house, I threw myself into my car. Somehow, I managed to pull back out of the driveway and began driving to the next drinking den.

Riding shotgun with me was another bottle of Jack Daniels. One of many problems in this experience was that I had drunk a good bit of 80-proof liquor so fast that the full effects from the alcohol hadn't fully kicked in.

I was a blackout drinker. Simply defined, a blackout drunk consumes such large amounts of alcohol that it interrupts the body's ability to form new memories. Afterward, the drinker often cannot remember where they were, who they were with, and what they were doing. It took me years of recovery to understand what was happening in my body and brain when I would drink like that.

Webster's Dictionary defines "alcohol" as a "volatile and flammable liquid that is the intoxicating agent in liquors. It is also used as a solvent in fuel." Yes, the same liquor anyone can buy from the grocery store is flammable and volatile.

The main ingredient in alcohol is ethanol. It is important to understand ethanol's effect on the body. As I was fading in and out of consciousness on my way to another party, this was happening in my body. When alcohol is ingested, ethanol begins slowing your brain down by locking up two receptors. Those receptors are GABA and NMDA. When the GABA receptor (neurotransmitter gamma-amino-butyric acid) is affected by ethanol, it inhibits your behavior by slowing down the neurotransmitter, and the body's response is to calm down and loosen up. The problem is exacerbated when a person drinks more alcohol than their body can metabolize, about 1 oz every hour.

Additionally, ethanol doesn't just block the GABA receptor. It also blocks the NMDA (N-methyl-D-aspartate receptor) receptor, making us tired and interfering with memory. When a person drinks too much alcohol and becomes intoxicated, the ethanol blocks the NMDA receptor, and they cannot recall events transpiring for extended periods. A person can be awake for hours, most likely acting a fool and doing things they'd never do when sober, and have no memory of what happened. This physiological swirl of alcohol and chemicals was what I was in the middle of while Jack Daniels rode shotgun.

While ethanol is causing those effects, it simultaneously causes our brain to release norepinephrine (a stress hormone) and adrenaline (also a stress hormone that increases blood circulation).

What else does the consumption of ethanol cause? The release of that feel-good chemical, dopamine. While all of this is happening, ethanol also jams up the neural pathways in our brain, which is why slurring of words, slow reaction times, trouble focusing, and trouble with balance are normal behaviors when a person consumes too much alcohol.

I had hammered down a dozen ounces of 80-proof liquor in under an hour. Remember, the average human body only metabolizes 1 oz of alcohol an hour. The full effects of all that craziness were ramping up in my internal world.

The next thing I recall after leaving one party en route to another was partially returning to my senses as a massive shot of adrenaline hit my body after I smashed into the back of an SUV stopped at a stoplight with a mom and her children inside. The wreck jolted me into some state of fuzzy consciousness, enough to panic and for me to immediately flee the scene.

I sped off and continued driving, and in my blurred lunacy, my phone rang. I answered to hear my mother say that someone wanted to talk to me. Heavily intoxicated, I slurred, "Sure, put them on." I had no idea what was happening. It was a police officer. After he informed me that someone had gotten my license plate as I sped away in my nearly totaled car. He suggested that I come home. I told him I would not be doing that because I had a party to go to.

Another moment of danger played out before I made it to the party. As I sped along a four-lane highway, the hood of my car flipped onto my windshield, preventing me from seeing the road. Somehow, I had the wherewithal to pull into the suicide lane, put my car in park, stumble out of my destroyed vehicle, and flip down my hood.

God often speaks to us in our circumstances and in more detail than we realize if we only pay attention. The fact that I had to pull my car into "the suicide lane" (the center lane of traffic that both sides use to turn) to flip the hood of my car down so that I could see was an accurate picture of my life. God was screaming for me to STOP before I killed myself or someone else.

I eventually made it to the party and finished my Jack Daniels, unwilling to answer my friends' questions about why the front end of my car looked like it had been through a meat grinder.

The next day was a rough one. I was deeply hungover, and for whatever reason, I decided it was best to turn myself in and face the consequences of my actions. I went to the police station and the front desk and said, "Aaah, I'm here to turn myself in for a crime I committed last night." No doubt, I looked like I could hardly open my eyes because I hardly could open my eyes.

The consequences? I was charged with a hit and run and given a court date. I then strolled out the front door of the police station, with which I was well acquainted, again with little consequences for my actions.

CHAPTER 8
An Addiction Warzone

RR

HAVE YOU EVER faced an issue that dragged on so long that you didn't even have the energy to think about overcoming it? I had created a mess so big that the thought of cleaning it up was so overwhelming that it paralyzed me with fear and anxiety.

The back-and-forth tension between wanting to live free and wanting to numb myself was the equivalent of myself and addiction going 12 rounds in a title fight, neither of us wanting to lose. The "suicide lane" debacle scared me straight for a couple of months, but when the underlying issues that drove me to darkness weren't addressed, they found their way back to the surface like a stowaway, searching for a new land of promise.

My unwillingness to surrender to the freedom that God had waiting for me left me in the maze of addiction. I kept believing that I could manage this beast. At times, I would try to cut back on my substance consumption, thinking I could somehow shoulder the weight of full-blown addiction while building a real life. All of these attempts failed and gave space for my addiction to worsen.

When alcohol left me incapable of holding down a job and brought me into trouble with the law, I decided the solution was to switch to another drug. I turned to smoking weed daily, idiotically thinking it would enable me to manage my deteriorating situation.

In recovery meetings, they call this *switching seats on the Titanic*. The point being the ship is sinking, but because of a lack of self-awareness and an impaired brain, the individual acts illogically and decides they can save themselves by simply switching seats on a sinking ship. In this instance, my attempt at switching seats was the equivalent of switching from a cozy armchair in my suite on the Titanic to sitting on the railing.

This is where the next demon is introduced into my life, OxyContin. Pills had been a prevalent visitor for years, but these pills were different. OxyContin is purer than just about all the heroin you'll find on the streets. Due to this drug's destruction in its wake, it is now highly regulated. Oxycodone is now the popular doctor-prescribed drug for severe pain. Very little OxyContin is found on the streets these days. But before this tiny pill was banned, it was the catalyst for well over a half million overdose deaths beginning in 1999.

In America's current phase of its drug addiction epidemic, Fentanyl has now taken the place of OxyContin. Fentanyl, an extremely high-powered opiate, is fifty times more potent than pure heroin. Yes, you read that correctly. If the death and destruction brought on by the grim reaper of OxyContin was bad (and it was horrific), imagine the destruction of a drug that's even cheaper, more accessible, and fifty times more potent than pure heroin can and will produce. As described on National Public Radio, "The annual overdose numbers hit an all-time high recently. According to the Centers for Disease Control and Prevention, more than 100,000 people died of a drug overdose from April 2020 to April 2021." Fentanyl has played a significant role in this epidemic.

I watched OxyContin roam the streets of Utah County and cities and communities across the country like a seasoned assassin. The devil lives in that drug, and he intends to use that drug to steal, kill, and destroy. I watched my friends drop like flies as this pill, dubbed a "miracle drug" by Purdue Pharma, killed people faster than the Vietnam War. In multiple years of this OxyContin epidemic, more people died in one year from overdose deaths than in the entire ten-year Vietnam War.

Eventually, Purdue Pharma was deemed criminally negligent in their claims about OxyContin. To date, they have paid billions of dollars to resolve thousands of lawsuits stemming from their involvement in the "Opioid Crisis" and their intentional profiting off addiction and death. The Sackler Family, the owners of Purdue Pharma, even paid billions out of their own personal wealth.

A New York Times article in May of 2020, citing the Justice Department, stated, "Purdue also paid kickbacks to providers to encourage them to prescribe even more of its products. CVS worked with Purdue Pharma, the maker of OxyContin, to offer promotional seminars on pain management to its pharmacists so they could reassure patients and doctors about the safety of the drug." An excellent documentary, "The Pharmacist," can be viewed on Netflix, and a book on these matters, "Dreamland," by author Sam Quinones, is also available.

Unfortunately, our streets were, and still are, a war zone. Drugs wreak havoc on communities. The argument has been and can be made that today's massive drug problem does as much damage to our nation as an actual war. The difference is that addiction is not forced on someone. War often is. This killer needs our agreement to do its dirty work. Once a person agrees to allow this assassin into their life, breaking free from the torment of drug and alcohol addiction can be every bit as grueling as trying to escape a maximum-security prison.

I know my mother often stayed up crying at night, wondering if she'd get a phone call from me in jail, or worse, stayed up anticipating a call relaying the horrifying message of my passing. How many mothers, fathers, wives, husbands, siblings, friends, and extended family members have experienced the same pain as the often-overlooked war prompted by drugs and addiction pummeled their communities and lives?

When the murderous "miracle drug," OxyContin, made its way into my world, I thought I'd found the perfect solution to calm my inner dissonance and to be productive. I didn't have to cover up my breath from the smell of alcohol. I didn't have to try to mask the smell of smoke on me from long sessions of smoking weed. I didn't have to waste lots of time getting high or drunk. With this new "miracle drug," I could slip into the bathroom at work, at school, or anywhere and snort a pill and, in moments, step right back out into the flow of everyday life.

However, there were other real and serious problems associated with OxyContin. The first problem was that using this drug was like playing Russian Roulette, and its effects were just as evident as the smell of alcohol and smoke. Second, Oxy was insanely expensive, often a dollar per milligram; as my tolerance quickly grew, I needed 80 milligrams a day, that's eighty dollars a day, to stay high. Additionally, OxyContin is highly addictive, beyond anything I had experienced. Even while I was in the middle of the euphoric waltz this drug induced in my mind, I would already start thinking about when the high would wear off and how I needed more. Additionally, after the climax of the euphoria leaves, you are still heavily sedated and left meandering through a cataclysmic wasteland while often convinced life is in perfect order.

I managed to save some money, get back in school, get a new girlfriend, and I was writing for the university newspaper. As far as I was concerned, my life was back in order. Falsely confident, I began telling myself I could start partying again, conning myself with the lie that I would be able to manage my drug use this time.

With some money in my pocket and feeling productive and in control again, I concluded that pills would have to be my one and only drug of choice this time. And so, my relationship with OxyContin began. As you notice, the relapse happened in my mind long before I acted on it. And, of course, it was no time at all before this drug possessed me. Once it did, it destroyed everything positive and good that I had gained in my short stint of white-knuckle sobriety.

I remember one incident during my season of Oxy-induced trances. I had to give a speech at my 9 a.m. Communications Class, but I didn't prepare for the speech. I didn't need to because I convinced myself that if I snorted a pill before giving the speech, I would be calm and charmingly brilliant in front of my captive college audience.

At this point in my downward spiral, I was, at least, still actually attending classes, and this was my first class of the day. After I pulled into the student lot and parked my car, I popped the tiny assassin in my mouth and sucked the time-release coating off the pill. Removing it from my mouth, I used my lighter to crush it into dust inside a dollar bill and snorted it up my nostril.

My heart rate slowed, and my senses were immediately filled with synthetic elation. As the morphine molecule entered my bloodstream and began to attach to my natural opioid receptors, a massive hit of dopamine infused my entire body. My pupils dilated. I went from being tired due to lack of sleep to instant euphoria.

Almost before I left my car, I felt like I was the spitting image of perfection. I waltzed across campus, feeling light as a feather yet heavy as a bulldozer. I floated my way into class, but then it hit me: the recognition and reality of my unpreparedness. That reality began to boost my heart rate. Sweat formed on my forehead, and I started to get the same feeling I used to get when the police questioned me.

I sat in class, waiting for my turn to speak. I watched the clock through droopy, sedated eyes, hoping against hope I would somehow escape the ensuing assignment. Suddenly, my name was called. I stood and drifted my way to the front of the class. I mumbled something, even though I was as high as Keith Richards on stage at a Rolling Stones concert.

I tried my best to speak eloquently, but the internal dialogue kept getting louder and louder. "Every single person in here knows you're high as a kite…You're fooling no one…You're making no sense," were the thoughts ringing through my head so loud that I was confident my classmates could hear it. I mumbled through my made-up speech, making sure that I mentioned that I wrote for the school newspaper in hopes of adding some clout to my words.

My short speech ended as I wiped the sweat off my forehead while looking pale as a ghost. As I sluggishly made my way down the aisle to my desk, I felt exposed as anxiety tried to creep into my current state of mind, but the high from the Oxy was still too strong to allow anxiety to settle in my mind.

I knew that this ride wouldn't last. Even as I chased the ever-elusive opiate high, I knew that this roller coaster would eventually come to a screeching halt. And it did.

In the coming season, as it always does, the house of cards I had constructed started crashing down. Shortly after that debacle, I dropped out of school. I ran out of money and couldn't afford Oxy anymore. It all happened in a matter of weeks. I went through the agony of opiate withdrawal, slightly mitigated because I went back to drinking. I was again on that vicious merry-go-round from which there seemed no escape.

The larger problem in all of this was that the weight of years of drug addiction and the self-loathing it brought was quickly becoming too much to bear. My brilliant solution? I decided, yet again, that if I switched things up and moved to a new city, I could start all over and avoid—rather than address—the issues tearing me apart. I chose a town in the middle of nowhere in southern Utah.

I thought that if I could hide from the world and start over, everything would magically return to normal. I was wrong again, but this time, the "rock bottom" I would face would produce a change beyond what I could ask, think, or ever possibly imagine.

CHAPTER 9
The End and The Beginning

RR

I WAS TWENTY-SIX YEARS old. I was defeated, depressed, and hanging on to the last thread at the end of a long rope. And I certainly had no idea that the reality of the following Bible verse was soon to begin unfolding in my disastrous life, "You are blessed when you are at the end of your rope. With less of you there is more of God and his rule." (Matthew 5:3, Message Bible)

As bad as my circumstances were, like many people who struggle with addiction, I was still able to put up enough of a facade that not everyone could see how bad things really were. However, by this point, even that counterproductive charade had lost its ability to deceive completely.

What did I do? I did what I always did: I ran away. I ran from my problems and my notorious reputation in the city I grew up in and landed in Cedar City, Utah. Yes, I'm aware that you've probably never heard of it. Few people have. It is in the southern half of Utah and has a population of under thirty thousand people.

By now, the "fun" of partying was gone. The girlfriends were gone. The money was gone. My dreams for any kind of an enjoyable, let alone productive, life were long gone. And sadly, I didn't have the mental fortitude to try and get any positivity or motivation back in my life.

Seeing as I was out of money and had no connections for drugs in that tiny area, I returned to the legal drug of alcohol. I spent my evenings staying up late, drinking massive amounts of whiskey. I had reached rock bottom in my life, and I knew it. The only thing I had left was depression, isolation, spiritual torment, and declining physical health.

However, I was still afraid to return to my old stomping grounds and "face the music." I thought it best to stay in Nowhere Ville, Utah, and continue running from my problems. I managed to find a rental room in an apartment, and I got a job working at a restaurant chain where I had previously worked. I lasted at the restaurant for roughly two weeks. Waiting tables required me to work in public, serving a variety of people, and that was too much to handle in my addiction-ridden state. With no job, fast food, and alcohol as my diet, my internal world and spiritual well-being were rotting away like fruit left in the hot sun. I was near the end, but I didn't know that yet.

One thing I knew was this: as I wandered through the dark maze, prayers were the guiding light that I didn't even know were still burning for me. When I really wanted to change, I knew they would help, and they always did. Whenever I expressed the desire to change or get help, they were there to assist. So, once again, desperate and out of all resources and options, I made a difficult phone call to my mom.

How my mom stayed strong, continued to pray for me, and kept hope that I would eventually change was an amazing miracle in and of itself. I remember calling her humiliated, engulfed in shame and guilt. My first words were, "Mom, I need help. Are you and Dad still willing to help me get into treatment?" She was understandably concerned and frustrated with me and my issues. Not only did I ask them to help me get some help, but I asked them to send me fifty dollars so I could make it home. "Erik, we will send you forty dollars," she explained, and then in a tone of stern love, "but if we find a rehab facility for you to go into in the next few days and you decide not to do so, you will have to leave."

I was relieved. They wired me the money, and I ran for help this time.

When we read the story of the Prodigal Son in the Bible, we read of a young man who takes his inheritance and runs off to waste it on partying and women. This young man had a good life. But he bought into the lie that there was a better life out there apart from God and his family. He requested his inheritance and ran off to a world he had been deceived into believing would provide him with a fairy tale existence.

My parents may not have handed me a large sum of money, but they handed me an inheritance of values and morals which, when wisely stewarded, will produce a wonderful life. My parents gave me everything I needed to succeed. They taught me right from wrong, they disciplined me the best they could, and they loved me. For this, I am blessed because this is obviously not everyone's experience growing up, but I took that valuable inheritance and ran off and squandered it and invested in my demise.

I was at my wit's end when it came to sanity. I had no license, no registration, no insurance, and at least a few warrants out for my arrest. There I was, again, looking for a way out of the insanely disastrous life I had created because of drug and alcohol abuse.

My thoughts were like a NASCAR race with speeding cars wildly circling a track but never going anywhere. The only thing that was certain at that moment was that my future was completely uncertain.

I had spent a long thirteen years on this treacherous path. I had watched over thirty of my friends die in one way or another from addiction. I just wanted the chaos to end. I wanted the roller coaster ride to stop so I could get off. And most of all, I longed for real peace.

On this evening, I exited the freeway and turned my car down a road with far less traffic. Moments later, a cop turned right behind me. Fear gripped me, and a shot of adrenaline coursed through my veins.

"How is this possible?! I've never seen a police officer on this road," I asked myself. I tried to nonchalantly speed up and make a turn, hoping the police officer wouldn't see my expired tags. He noticed my unusual acceleration, and those menacing yet freeing blue and red flashing lights lit up behind me for the last time.

It was a miracle I was sober and did not have drugs in my possession as I pulled over on that quiet back street. I instantly lit up a cigarette and chain-smoked through my entire encounter. I knew I was going to jail, and smoking was not allowed in that concrete jungle.

But something was distinctly different. It was as if time slowed to a crawl. I felt a peace and strange confidence about the future as I engaged in this all too familiar routine of being arrested. I was exhausted, completely defeated, and I nearly screamed out, "Please, just help me!" Thirteen years of living amongst the walking dead had taken its toll on me. As the officer approached the window, I was already waving the white flag of surrender. I had been arrested many times before, yet none of those times did I feel the internal shift that was taking place in my consciousness as it did at that moment. Before the officer could even ask for my license, registration, and insurance, I had made up my mind.

He came to my window, and I handed him my expired license in full surrender, "Here you go. I have no license, registration, or insurance, and I have multiple warrants for my arrest." He was visibly surprised to hear a raw dose of honesty and nearly smiled as he said, "Ok, just wait here and sit tight." Another squad car soon pulled onto the scene as time moved slowly. And as I sat there, my mind experienced a moment of clarity—amazing because clarity was nearly nonexistent in my world.

I sat with glimpses of peace and memories of misery in my smoke-filled car and thought to myself, "I'm heading to my parents to get help, I'm completely defeated, I'm beyond tired, and I'm out of options... God, please help me." I suppose I knew I wasn't just thinking those words; I was praying. Deep down in my soul, I inherently knew that the only way out of the internal dungeon I was enslaved was to fully surrender to God and ask Him for His help.

I'm sure the length of my prayer didn't rouse His heart, nor did its eloquence. My prayer was short and anything but elegant. But it was sincere. And I believe it was the posture of my heart that moved God's heart. I didn't have the energy to juggle any more lies. I was honest, and I was candid with God. I couldn't do life alone anymore. I wanted and needed Him.

Moments later, late on that quiet Friday night, the police officer and his partner came, slapped the cuffs on me, and hauled me off to jail. I had a long weekend in an 8-man holding cell.

I recall sitting in jail, looking around and saying, "This isn't me. I don't belong here." Of course, I did. I had broken the law. However, I tried to talk some sense into myself from the deepest place in my heart. You may think you can't escape the imprisonment of addiction, but you certainly can. You may think you are the sum total of your bad choices, but when God steps on the scene of your life, He rewrites the story. And God did not create you for addiction. He made you to walk in freedom and live in His peace.

I sat in my jail attire and listened to the stories of the other inmates and why they got arrested. I listened as they bragged about how much dope they were doing, all their connections, and how they would beat the system the next time they got out. I had participated in those conversations in past visits to jail, but it had no appeal to me this time.

I wasn't better than anyone in there. I was right where I belonged. Those conversations, which are constant conversations that inmates have in jail, suddenly left a foul taste in my mouth. This time, I was ready to face the truth because I knew exactly where my old way of doing things had always taken me. From the depths of my empty, lonely, dark, and dreary soul, I cried out and admitted I was done. I gave up trying to fight a fight I could not win alone.

Monday morning in jail can't come soon enough. That's when court appointments start. Like clockwork, I was hauled off to court to see the judge, decked out in fabulous jail fashion, sporting shiny bracelets. I shuffled into the courtroom that Monday morning, expecting to have a list of consequences dished out to me, and rightfully so. My name was called. That was always a shameful moment, having your name disgracefully broadcast for all to hear.

She looked at me, and she looked over my file. Then she said, "You have two options. One, we let you go today, and you must deal with your past consequences and the new ones you have just acquired by reporting to probation and entering outpatient treatment. Or two, you go to jail for two weeks, and we wipe your slate clean."

I had been in front of many judges and received many consequences, and, honestly, most of them I avoided as soon as I left the courtroom.

This time, I was shocked. I expected a lengthy probation period, a few new fines, more jail time, and another mountain of problems to solve. I responded without thinking, as I had done most of my life. I quickly announced, "I'll go to jail."

CHAPTER 10
A New Life Begins

RAR

ONE OF THE reasons I adamantly avoided the painful process of change was that I had no idea how to change. Deep in the abyss of my pain-filled heart, I knew I would have to admit I was completely wrong. Additionally, I would have to humble myself and take direction. That's hard to do when pride and ego are the fuel on which your vehicle runs.

I didn't want to admit to anyone that I didn't have life all figured out, even though everyone but me already knew it. I wanted to be in control, and surrendering to God and submitting to the process of growth and recovery was an admission and declaration that I was clueless and needed help.

I had no idea how to manage my life, let alone live drug and alcohol-free. The Good News was that God was and is in the business of taking people who are written off as failures, grabbing hold of their lives, and transforming them into victorious trophies of His grace. As Psalm 113:7-8 *explains, "He promotes the poor, picking them up from the dirt, and rescues the needy from the garbage dump. 8 He turns paupers into princes and seats them on their royal thrones of honor." (Passion Translation)*

A few days after being released from the Utah County Jail, my mom dropped me off at the Salt Lake City Airport. I can still visualize the look on her face, having accumulated years of stress because of my rebellion yet still possessing a sliver of hope. It was as if a question was visibly written on her face, "Will he actually change this time?" I said my goodbyes with a tiny bit of hope and boarded the plane to Seattle.

I took this gift as seriously as I could. I was afraid, but I started trying. This time was different. It was different because I desperately relied on God, the same God that had torched me in His fiery presence on multiple occasions in previous years. The same God that saw fit to spare my life numerous times, and the same God with a plan and purpose for my life.

I was picked up at the Seattle Airport and driven deep into the woods for a few hours to a lovely house. It was already a glorious upgrade from the living situations I was accustomed to. Treatment centers can be strange places. For a moment, let's set aside the fact that everyone coming to rehab desperately needs to embrace a healing process for their physical, mental, and spiritual well-being. In treatment, you find people who want recovery, people who are forced there by loved ones, the courts, or their work, and mixed into all that, you have people who frequent treatment centers just to dry out for a while and then jump right back onto the merry-go-round of addiction.

I was there willingly in an attempt to live. I was as ready as I would ever be to change. I dove in and got started. I woke up early and read and wrote and prayed. I participated in group sessions. About fifteen of us were there at that time, as this was a fairly new treatment center. Even when my issues surfaced, and I disobeyed the rules on more than one occasion, I honestly wanted recovery.

One of the things that immediately began to pay dividends for me was being in a community with like-minded people with whom I could build relationships. This was new for me. Isolation and unhealthy relationships were my norm, as they are for everyone struggling with addiction.

I began learning how to live this new life. One powerful thing I learned was that our bodies are created to thrive in healthy relationships.

When we are not in healthy relationships, it negatively affects our chemical makeup.

As I previously shared, drugs and alcohol force our body to produce the feel-good chemicals dopamine and serotonin. However, our bodies naturally produce these feel-good chemicals when living life in healthy connection with other people and developing healthy relationships.

Ask yourself this: Have you ever been lonely, isolated, and noticeably felt terrible? Then maybe thoughts like the following began stirring in your mind, "Why does everyone else seem to have it figured out? What is wrong with me? Why hasn't so-and-so called me? My life is so boring and lame!" I knew this negative insanity all too well. It was my culture for years. Now, think about this: after being divided and isolated for a prolonged time, have you ever noticed that you feel better almost immediately after a hug and enjoyable or positive conversation with a friend or family member?

Here is what happens when we push past our invisible walls of fear and isolation. Humans are created to connect with others, and when we are connected, our brain rewards us for it. There's nothing wrong with wanting to feel good. The question is, are we going about trying to feel good in positive and beneficial ways?

Research has shown that when we experience a hug from a friend or a warm conversation, our brain releases a chemical known as the "bonding hormone" or the "love hormone." As explained at DignityHealth.com, this chemical is called Oxytocin, and it "stimulates the release of other feel-good hormones, such as dopamine and serotonin, while reducing stress hormones, such as cortisol and norepinephrine."

The feel-good chemicals that combat the negative effects of stress chemicals are released in our bodies when we spend time around others and work on establishing healthy and close connections with people. Simply living connected with people in close, healthy relationships is one of the most important keys to experiencing feel-good chemicals flowing regularly, naturally, and healthily through your body.

That's great news in and of itself, but there is more. On one end of the spectrum, we have Oxytocin, which fires up your dopamine and serotonin, making you feel good. On the opposite end of the spectrum is a chemical that our body produces called Tachykinin (Tack-ee-kine-in).

Many people have this demoralizing chemical flowing through their blood, and they don't even know it or know what it is.

Tachykinin is the chemical our body produces when we experience extended periods of isolation and disconnectedness. This devilish disconnector not only thrives in isolation, but when Tachykinin has been flowing through our body for an extended period, it tricks our brain into thinking that isolation is best for us. Neuroscience educator, Staci Danford, elaborated on this as a guest on my podcast, The Recovering Reality Podcast.

I recall numerous times, while in dark seclusion, being overrun with thoughts of, "No one cares anyways." "I can do this on my own." "Nothing I do succeeds anyway." "It's better that I'm alone." As the cunning culprit, Tachykinin, flowed through my system, the devil himself pounced at the chance to drive me to live entirely disconnected from the very thing I needed most: healthy connections with other people.

When the chemical Tachykinin floods your system, it furthers pain and isolation, destroys hope, and discourages healthy relationships. In such situations, we then need to do exactly the opposite of what our brain and body are telling us to do. Just like love conquers fear, we need to replace Tachykinin with healthy relationships with others.

Of course, I knew none of this as I sleep-walked through my previous rehab experience and years of addiction. But as I began connecting with people, showing up in life, and honestly trying, my level of hope started increasing. With hope came newfound strength, and as I desperately cried out, received God's help, and started putting one foot in front of the other, I slowly began to live connected, and the healing process began.

With clarity and hope surfacing, I began to get glimpses into how blurred my vision of life had been.

Have you ever worn a pair of glasses that were the wrong prescription? After even a few seconds of wearing those glasses, your eyes throb, your headaches, and everything you do is affected. The more I prayed, read my Bible, studied recovery books, wrote about my feelings and the recovery process, and tried my best to be connected to God and people, the more my vision cleared. It was like having spiritual Lasik eye surgery. Except this time, my Doctor was the best ever. Indeed, He is so good and great that one of His names is "The Great Physician."

For years, I had crawled through a barren desert, and in doing so, I nearly died of spiritual dehydration. This rehab in the woods brought me to a lifesaving oasis, and God was the long drink of crystal-clear cold water I desperately needed. I wanted to know God and if He really is who He says He is.

While opening myself up to God, I also came to believe I should not live in Utah any longer, if for no other reason than to break clean from the associations and influences still there. God was speaking to me, and I felt that the only way I would survive would be to leave my old stomping grounds. I had an aunt and uncle in San Diego, and some of the staff from the treatment center lived in San Diego. They told me that there was a big recovery community in Southern California.

I finished my stint in Seattle and hopped a plane back to Utah with far more hope than when I landed in Seattle one month earlier. It was a good start, but it wasn't all cupcakes and rainbows when I landed in Utah. It felt eerie. It still felt like death to me. Even getting off the plane and driving through Salt Lake City and into Utah County, there was nowhere I looked that didn't remind me of my past insanity. I couldn't shake it. It was like my mind was a canvas, and pictures and movie reels were brought back to my vision, accompanied by shame and guilt.

There's a term in the index of recovery lingo that defines what happens in our mind when we encounter a painful or unwanted moment or season from our past. That term is "trigger." I was constantly triggered as we embarked on the forty-five-minute drive from the airport to my parents' house.

I was trying to get back to normal life. The power of God hadn't set me entirely free yet, and Post Traumatic Stress Disorder (PTSD) was tormenting me. I didn't know how to deal with these "triggers," so I did my best with what I had. And as most people will testify, addiction is hard to beat. For starters, less than ten percent of people who struggle with addiction get the professional help they need. Many people struggle with addiction for years, or even decades, before they finally get into a treatment program. Statistically, more than two-thirds of individuals in recovery relapse within months, if not weeks, of beginning addiction treatment.

Part of the problem is that treatment centers are controlled environments. It's not difficult to stay clean and sober in an in-patient rehab program, although it is often a needed step to start the journey. In treatment, you learn about the mindsets and tools needed to live in recovery. My problem was that I didn't fully understand how to use any of the strategies and tools because I hadn't had the opportunity to apply them in real life yet.

Thirty days in treatment does not cure addiction; far from it. Thirty days of treatment is like being told how to swim, being shown films on how to swim, and then being thrown into the deep end and expected to swim. In rehab, you sit with others and study for thirty days in a carefully structured environment.

I was back in real life, and I had a problem. I always ran from real life, but it was no more running this time. No more hiding. It was time to face life. It was time to figure out what an actual relationship with God looked like. It was time to try to foster that relationship. It was time to grow up and stop running, and it was time to stop playing the victim and start being responsible.

We arrived back at my parents' house, and immediately, my mind fought my heart to get as high as possible. This was where I realized that the more I tried to avoid anything that made me uncomfortable, the more I avoided personal growth. This is true for the flip side as well. The more I stepped into doing things that made me uncomfortable, the more comfortable I became in my own skin. It's a paradoxical paradise.

I can't tell you why I moved to San Diego, California, other than it felt right. I talked with my aunt and uncle, the same aunt and uncle I went to live with for a few months after getting in trouble in ninth grade, hoping to get my life in order. They agreed to let me live there for two months until I got on my feet. But the first thing on the agenda to put this in motion was having to check in with the court one last time and update them on my status since getting out of treatment.

I was told in treatment that honesty was an essential requirement for living a life of real change. I got some advice from a trusted friend. They convinced me to write the judge a letter before my court appearance. I wrote a one-page letter to the judge explaining that I was done with my past life and my plan was to move to California, seek God, and get sober by going to Alcoholics Anonymous.

In past appearances before the court, I often dressed like I was heading to a party afterward. Not this time. I wore khakis, a collared shirt, and a tie this time. I remember that day. I was very nervous because I was making this appearance without chemicals calming my nerves this time.

Seeing and entering the court triggered memories of handcuffs, warrants, fines, shame, and the list goes on. My old identity lingered, but I was learning my new identity in God this time. When my name was called in court, my heart rate shot up like the upbeat beginning of a techno song. I stood and explained to the judge that I did my time in jail, and upon being released, I spent thirty days in a treatment center in Seattle.

I then handed the bailiff the letter I had written and told the judge that my plan was spelled out within that page. She took a moment to read it, and what took a minute or so felt like an hour or more to me. I had a twenty-minute conversation in my head during that one minute. "You're an idiot. She isn't going to believe you. You've lied to her every time you've talked with her before. Why is she going to believe anything in that letter?" The voice of doubt made some legitimate points. But a different voice was at work in my life this time. God was now working in my life as a voice of faith.

Suddenly, the judge interrupted my internal conversation with her decree, "Yes, you can go." I didn't know I needed the judge's permission. I thought they had wiped my slate clean. Either way, I was shocked. And whether she was saying, "Yes, you can go." or "Yes! Get out of my city and never come back!" I knew I had been dealt the best hand possible.

Looking back, I understand that the truth of that moment was I had surrendered my life to Jesus, and the verdict over my life became "not guilty."

I was off to California.

CHAPTER 11
Learning to Crawl

ЯⱯЯ

Most people have probably heard the term "born-again Christian," but I can say that at this time in my journey with God, I had not heard the term. To the best of my recollection, I don't recall hearing it used in Mormon-dominated Utah.

Some people might set out to go to church and learn more about Jesus in an attempt to make themselves a good person. This was not me. I certainly wanted to be a better person, but at this point, I was just trying not to die, not to go to any more rehabs, and not spend any more time in jail. I flung myself into God's arms out of a desire to live. Becoming some sort of studious and upright religious churchgoer was not my aim.

But the biblical term "born again" caught my attention. It comes straight from the mouth of Jesus in the third chapter of the Gospel of John when an inquisitive religious leader named Nicodemus searches out Jesus in the secrecy of night. Shortly into their discussion on religious matters, Jesus explains to him the mandatory need to be "born again."

Interestingly, "born again" can be as accurately translated as "born from above." This made much more sense to me. When my eyes were opened to the fact that as I revealed my heart to God, new life would enter my heart in the form of the Spirit of God, it made sense. I was dead inside. I needed to be *born again from above*.

It was during this window of time I began to ask God lots of questions.

One of those questions was, "How do I get this craziness out of my life for good?" I had moved from Utah to California, changed phone numbers, and I was doing some things differently. But I was about to learn a hard lesson. *Pretending a problem isn't there does not make it go away*. Let me explain. Have you ever heard the expression, "Time heals all wounds?" This is not true. If this were true, then traumatic childhoods should have no hold on grown adults, especially after long passages of time.

Elevating time as some magic healer is akin to having a huge cut on your arm that needs stitches and medical assistance and telling everyone to ignore it and give it some time. Does pretending a massive gash on your arm isn't there make it just go away? I think not. If you ignore it, you likely run the risk of it getting infected. If so, the infection could spread and eventually leave a huge scar. Worse yet is the possibility of sepsis (the body's response to an infection, as it damages its tissue or turns on its own body, leading to severe organ damage or possibly death). My wounds from addiction had infected my life. The infection had spread into all areas, and there were scars on my heart and my psyche.

When we hear the term "time heals all wounds," it almost always refers to the wounds our hearts endure. However, while time can be an element of healing when the wound is adequately addressed, time, in and of itself, will not heal a person's deep wounds. Treating our internal wounds is much better by accessing God's power through Christ, our Great Healer.

When I left Utah, my heart was riddled with scars, but simultaneously, it was set on the hope that my future didn't have to look like my past. So, with my whole life packed into my car, I set off for San Diego, California. This time, I was not running from something. This time, I was running towards something.

I arrived in San Diego at my aunt and uncle's house just two blocks from the beach in Carlsbad, California, in early 2009. I had gone from jail and rehab just weeks before being sober and living in a nice house within walking distance of the beach. God was already showing me that His kindness *was leading me to repentance.*

There was an issue working against me, though. I didn't fully understand the importance of not delaying the healing process. I went to some Alcoholics Anonymous meetings and spent some time praying, but I avoided facing the big internal issues before me, thinking they would go away on their own. They didn't because time doesn't heal us; God does.

Here I was, living at my aunt and uncle's house, hoping I could coast my way into freedom from addiction, but after being at their house for a couple of weeks, old habits began itching at me in the form of reminiscences of the good old days. These thoughts started bouncing around in my mind like demons on pogo sticks. If that itch to get high or drunk isn't scratched the right way, then the old methods of scratching that damning itch will eventually start playing themselves out again. And that is what happened. It started in my mind and then finally played out in my actions.

One day, when no one was home, I *thought* searching my aunt and uncle's house for painkillers would be a good idea. I didn't plan on taking the painkillers, mind you, at least at that exact moment. I was curious if they had any in case I changed my mind. Subconsciously, I had already relapsed.

I knew exactly where to look around the house, and sure enough, I found an old bottle of Lortabs. I didn't take any that day, and for that, I was proud of myself. But I always knew where they were if/when I changed my mind.

In recovery, this is called a "reservation." It's kind of like this: say I know that I'm going to eat at home with my family tonight, but I have an inkling the meal might not be as good as I'd like it to be. So, just in case, I make a reservation to go out to eat that night at a place where I want to eat. I may not go and use the reservation that night, but eventually, I'll skip out by myself and eat where I want to eat and what I want to eat outside of relationships and connections to other people.

Seeing as a relapse had already happened in my mind, it only took a couple of weeks for it to happen in my actions. The stage was set, and the scene began to play out when I connected to an old friend. I didn't know it, but this friend had moved to Los Angeles. After a brief conversation, we decided that I would drive up to Los Angeles and see her for a night.

If you have a good recovery community and support system, this is the moment when you stop and think about where this decision will lead you. If the temptation remains, then you call someone else in recovery, a mentor who is there to support you through challenging times.

Understanding that I was going to see a friend was not, in and of itself, a life-or-death-threatening decision regarding addiction. The real issue, the deeper issue, was my inability to know how to do life sober and keep myself out of situations that caused me to want to drink and use drugs. I still didn't know how to be sober and have real conversations and relationships with people, especially females. I especially didn't know how to be with women from my past with whom I had gotten high or drunk. In these circumstances, the puppet master of addiction walked me back onto that dark merry-go-round.

I should have called for reinforcements; I didn't do that. I had decided what I would do weeks prior when I searched for painkillers in my aunt and uncle's bathroom cabinet. The same thinking that led me into thirteen years of destructive addiction was the same thinking that led me to try again to mask my pain behind a false facade of being capable and in control. However, I knew exactly what I was doing. That's why I didn't tell anyone, because they would have tried to talk me out of it. My mind was made up, and trying to stop me at that point would have been like trying to stop a runaway train.

The next thing I told myself after I decided to spend the night in Los Angeles was that, of course, I couldn't go sober. I further rationalized that I couldn't drive two hours to Los Angeles while drinking. So, my solution was to fulfill the "reservation" I made a couple of weeks previously with a bottle of Lortabs.

I found the bottle and emptied five chaotic candies into my hand. They felt like cinder blocks and comfortable cushions at the same time. Cinder blocks because I knew the weight of my decision, but comfortable cushions because I knew the feeling that awaited me once I pulled the pin on the grenade. I ate a handful of pills and slipped back into the euphoria of chemical romance.

Thirty minutes into my two-hour drive to Los Angeles, I was glad I was wearing my seatbelt because I was beginning to feel like I was floating. I was doing eighty miles an hour on the freeway as I became reacquainted with my old counterfeit friend, Euphoria.

I had forgotten how comfortable this peaceful poison made me feel, at least for a few hours. I was swerving in and out of traffic on Southern California's I-5 freeway like it was a video game.

Even a quiet night with my friend and I couldn't stop the sickness. Before my eyelids closed that night in her apartment, the promise of peace that painkillers lured me with began to turn on me. Mental and physical sickness ensued. The total weight of shame and guilt hit me with the force of a river bursting through a dam. My chemically induced high had worn off, and physical and spiritual sickness engulfed me like a wet blanket. Crippling regret over my relapse and the terror of an uncertain future had me wishing that once I fell asleep, it would be for good. I was back in familiar darkness.

Morning came all too quickly, and my eyes opened like stones being rolled away from a tomb with a rotting corpse inside. I just wanted to hide under the blanket and drift away from this world, but I had to face the music. I got up, said my goodbyes, and made the drive of shame back to San Diego.

Less than twenty minutes into my drive, I called my friend Eileen to tell her I had relapsed. Eileen is a saint; she was on staff at my last treatment center. She listened to me, judgment-free, and encouraged me that I could still live free from addiction.

In the past, I never called and told people about terrible choices I had made the night before and the deep regret I felt in doing so. Calling Eileen was a new act of accountability, and the new me was rising to the surface. And while I was inching towards the reality of freedom, God didn't up and leave me just because I screwed up. It was His grace that empowered me to make that call.

Still, those wicked whispers kept chattering to me on my long drive home. The whole way home, all I could think about was Vodka. Not because I liked the taste or wanted to drink it. I hated it. But I knew it would numb some of the pain within my soul.

I made it home and hid in my room under my blanket. I slept the day away and the night, too. When I woke up the next day, I had a choice. I could face the pain and get back on the right track, or run from it, numb it, and throw my life away. I chose option two and drove straight to the liquor store. The biblical promise in Proverbs 23:21 is, "Drunks and gluttons will end up on skid row, in a stupor and dressed in rags" (Message Bible), and that message was about to write its final chapter in my life.

In my pain, I just wanted some joy, peace, and energy that didn't destroy my life. Why couldn't I live free? Why was this happening? What was wrong with me? These were the questions I asked myself as I drove to the liquor store in search of medication. I got there, knowing it was wrong and not wanting to do it, but I went in and grabbed a cheap pint of Vodka, paid for it, took it out, and sat in my car.

I ran through every mental stop sign that popped into my head, cracked the top, and took a big swig. The unattractive aftertaste was close to flames coming out of my mouth, and the deceptively attractive warmth that hit my belly felt like coal being tossed into the furnace of my heart during a cold winter night. I hated it, but I loved it. I was terrified but energized. I was lost but trying to find myself in the bottle again.

I did nothing but drink and sit by the beach for the rest of the day. I drove home intoxicated and went straight to my room. I went right back to drinking every day. A few days later, I grabbed my empty vodka bottles and put them on my bed with my backpack. I ran out the door and left the empty bottles on the bed in a hurry to get somewhere. Not only that, I left my bedroom door open.

What happened? My uncle found them and was waiting to talk to me when I got home.

CHAPTER 12
His Kindness Led Me to Change

RR

I QUICKLY LEARNED THROUGH experience that God's way of ushering change into my heart would be through His kindness, not punishment. It was a foreign reality in which I was getting a crash course. The idea that God truly loved me and had a good plan for my life was all new to me.

How on earth is the idea that God loves us knowable? How was I supposed to honestly know and believe that God loves me? Did I think happy thoughts all day? Was I supposed to believe and then experience it, or was I supposed to experience and then believe it? These were questions I had.

I was starting to get more clarity into the reality that there was clearly a power at work in my life that was much greater than me. God was determined to love the "hell" out of me.

Most importantly, the magnificent understanding of what Christ did on the cross began to settle in my heart. That's when I started catching a glimpse of God's glorious love and the freedom He offers each of us. But first, I needed to know that God wasn't disgusted with me. I needed to know He saw something valuable and lovable in me, even in the depths of my brokenness. Christ went to the cross for me because He loved and valued me and willingly paid the price for my redemption and freedom before I knew I needed it. *Romans 5:8 teaches us, "But God demonstrates His own love toward us, in that while we were still sinners, Christ died for us." (NKJV)*

For years, I believed the consequences of my actions occurred because God was punishing me for my imperfections and short-comings. Was I being punished by God all those times I broke the law and did the wrong thing? Or, had I blatantly disobeyed the law and, therefore, suffered the natural consequences of my actions?

I recall thinking that God was punishing me on more than one occasion. I can look back now and concede that God was disciplining me many times long before I realized it. The consequences I created were a result of my actions. It was coming to recognize God's mercy during all these times that finally won me over.

So, when my uncle sat me down, showed me the empty vodka bottles, and told me I had two days to go, I had nothing to say but, "You're right. I'll go." "Where am I going?" was the next question.

At this time, I was left with nothing. It was no one's fault but my own. I was again immersed in pain and self-recrimination, the inevitable consequences of my actions, and I had nowhere to go.

My life could have taken a dark and terrible turn at that moment, as it had many times before. But I had taken some baby steps and was at least open to allowing God in my life. Don't misunderstand me. God is always there for us. He had always been there for me as He is for you. However, He respects our freedom to choose. And it is when we are honest and open to His presence that He will employ a myriad of ways to love us into our true identity and purpose. I not only needed but was open to an authentic experience of His mercy and grace taking root in my life.

There was something else I needed to understand. I have talked with many people over the years who, for some reason, think that once they begin following God, their transformation is now largely dependent upon their efforts. They believe that when they were lost in "sin," grace saved them, but once they turned and started following God, their rescue was less dependent upon His grace and more on their efforts.

This is a misunderstanding on our part. It is true that God is not okay with each of us choosing to live however we want. Or doing whatever we want when He has provided us counsel and guidance as to what choices and actions will bring us joy and peace. Yet, the fact remains that no matter what I do, His love for me is constant, and His grace will never leave me. When I am weak, He is strong. His goal is to love me into wholeness in all seasons of my life.

Titus 3:4-6 states, "When the extraordinary compassion of God our Savior and his overpowering love suddenly appeared in person, as the brightness of a dawning day, he came to save us. Not because of any virtuous deed that we have done but only because of his extravagant mercy. He saved us, resurrecting us through the washing of rebirth. We are made completely new by the Holy Spirit, whom he splashed over us richly by Jesus, the Messiah, our Life Giver. (TPT)

God's grace and love acted like a wrecking ball against the walls I had built around my heart. Before I even started packing my stuff to leave my aunt and uncle's house, my cousin and her husband, knowing my poor decisions and the seriousness of my situation, said I could live with them until I got my feet under me. Their gracious offer to me was amazing. However, my cousin and her husband were also leaving to go out of town for a week, just a couple of days after I moved my few belongings into their spare bedroom.

What did I do? I kept drinking. I defaulted to the thinking and acting that was ingrained within me. I drank, and I drank, and I drank. What did God do? He loved me, and He loved me, and He loved me. He was not okay with my actions, but He is Love. He doesn't change. His unending love is what changes us.

My uncle started calling me a few days into this vicious cycle of isolation. When I didn't answer his calls, he showed up and began knocking on the front door. Adrenaline hit my veins as I lay on the couch drunk with a bottle of Bacardi in hand. I just wanted to be left alone. I just wanted to hide. But God was intent on loving me. So, when I heard the knock on the door, I ran to the back room and tried to hide under the bed.

My uncle came around back and began trying to come in through the window as I was still trying to fit my six-foot-two-inch, two-hundred-and-twenty-pound body under a tiny single-frame bed. The winds of shame blew a dark cloud over me, and the familiar storm of guilt began its downpour. I was still trying to hide from people, and I foolishly tried to hide from God. I still thought I could manage my mess and figure life out on my own.

I got up from the ground and went to the front door. That's precisely what God wanted me to do. He wanted me to open the door and let Him and the people that loved me inside. When I opened the door, my cousins and uncle stared at me. And I stared back at them drunk. Just like before, it was time to go.

I wandered in my self-inflicted shame the following day, now sober and hungover. The only conclusion in my mind was, "I was an unfixable problem." And you probably would agree with that assessment. The years of sinking into addiction had simply made me a slow learner.

But then, whether it was mercy or desperation, I made a call. I called my only friend left in Southern California, Eileen. Whenever I reached out to her for help, she gave me more help than I could have imagined. When I explained my situation, she told me about the cheapest sober living home she knew of in Orange County and gave me the number. I called, and they said if I passed a drug test, I could move into the old (emphasis on old) hotel turned sober living home. I began driving from San Diego to Orange County, and on the road, I called my sister and her husband and begged for the money needed for the first week of rent. They said they would help for one week. Again, God's grace was there to catch me when I fell.

How deep can a person dig the hole before God says, "Enough, I'm done with you?" In Psalm 139:8, King David spoke the truth perfectly when he said, "If I make my bed in Sheol, behold, You are there." (Sheol is a word for the underworld, where wicked people descend at death.) I knew what I had to do, and I knew that God was the solution to my drug and drinking problems and that AA would help me along the way.

Upon arriving at my new residence, I quickly realized that this particular "sober living home" probably had more sober cockroaches than it did sober people. An old, dirty, and small seven-bedroom hotel blocks from the beach, with bunk beds in each room, had become my new living quarters. It reminded me more of a dope house than a safe haven. It smelled like what I imagined a house from the TV show "Hoarders" smelled like. The few rooms were divided into half-male and half-female living quarters. The company was less than desirable— but let's be honest, I was less than desirable at the time. Yet this was right where I needed to be for my eyes to be opened and for my mind to realize that I needed to drop the shovel and stop digging the hole I was hell-bent on deepening.

My only option was to keep trying. So that's what I did, I tried. I went to some A.A. meetings. I prayed daily and asked God to do what I could not do for myself. And honestly, what faith I had at this point was only that of a mustard seed. Small and fragile, but desperately real. At times, it felt like I was living in a military fort under constant attack, and all I could do was brace myself for the assault. I was in over my head. The spiritual battle I was stuck in because addiction was a battle for my soul was one I couldn't win by myself. Not because I hadn't tried, I had tried. But I was trying to win against the devil by employing my strength when I needed the cavalry, led by God Himself, to come to my rescue.

Life at this sober living home was certainly not The Ritz. It was more like the *Hotel California,* described in the Eagles song. It was desperate people trying to act as if they were not desperate. It was hurting people talking about how their lives weren't that bad. The conversations were about the big things the residents wanted to do with their lives, but those were steps they would start taking tomorrow. It was so easy to see through their self-delusion and hypocrisy. And it made me realize how easy it must have been for everyone to see through mine.

A week passed, and I begged my sister and her husband to pay for one more week of rent. They agreed, but they said it would be the last time. I had somehow managed to stay sober while trying to find a job, but I had found nothing. I had no money. I had nowhere to go. But God continued to show me, "*Where sin abounds, grace abounds all the more.*"

At the *Hotel California,* my racing thoughts of impending doom were interrupted by a phone call. I was used to phone calls that presented me with bad news, but a new trend was unveiling itself in my life. Good News was starting to find its way into my life. The call was from Eileen, and she had a question.

Eileen asked me, "Erik, my boyfriend, and I will both be out of town for a couple of weeks. Want to come house sit for us?" I specifically recall my response, "Eileen, you know that I'm like ten days sober, and you're asking me to come stay at your house, by myself, ten minutes from the beach, for two weeks, right?"

"I know, you told me this already," she calmly replied. She continued, "If you get high or drunk while we are gone, then when we get back, you gotta go. If you stay sober while we're gone, then when we get back, we can talk about the possibility of you renting our spare room for a while as you get your feet under you." I immediately replied, "Ok, when should I come?"

Why was this help coming to me? I certainly didn't deserve it. However, in my brokenness, I genuinely needed/asked for help. Many people think that in order to partake of God's goodness, we must clean ourselves up and then come to Him. The problem with that thinking is that this is impossible to do. I can't heal myself, fix myself, or clean myself. We need God to help us to do that. I just needed to continue seeking Him.

I simply had to throw myself at His feet in the middle of my filthy brokenness, and He was there to help me clean myself up. He wasn't shocked that I didn't do everything perfectly from the start. He's spent eons of time working with people who commit to Him, then backslide. But His solution was in place long before my problems even existed, and He was there through all the forward and backward steps I took. He is The Solution. He is "The Helper."

I packed my few belongings faster than a starving teenage boy hitting a buffet line. I drove from Orange County to Oceanside in San Diego County with a slight wind of hope beginning to blow against the dark clouds that followed me. I got to their house and met Eileen's boyfriend, Darin, for the first time. Darin is still a dear friend to this day. He has a heart of gold, but he can be rough around the edges sometimes—many of us can. He is five foot ten inches tall with an average build. He rides his Harley around with a smile and hosts a big goatee.

When we met, he was a handful of years into his recovery. He is a hard worker who survived decades of addiction. His occasional brashness can be deceiving because I quickly learned he is incredibly gracious, kind, and generous. He and Eileen were the hands and feet of God in my life for a number of years.

And to put things in perspective, as he met me for the first time, he gave me the keys to his house for two weeks. He seemed a bit concerned, rightfully so, but he trusted Eileen's judgment and God's plan. He let me into the house and showed me the spare upstairs room where I would stay. We then went out back, and each smoked a cigarette for a few minutes, and then he hit the road. Eileen had already left on her trip, so there I was with the house all to myself.

Long story short, I stayed sober. And upon this gracious couple's return home, I began to dive deep into recovery. My wonderful friends Darin and Eileen, acting under God's inspiration and as His instrument in my life, said I could stay for a while for minimal rent. A week later, I found a job and worked thirty-plus hours weekly.

At this point, I had far more questions than answers, but as I worked at recovery one day at a time, I began to see hope rising. Darin and Eileen loved me and talked about their journeys and recovery with me daily. They had been there, and they knew what I was going through, and that alone was huge—and another sign of God's grace active in my life. Further, when my first paycheck came, these two wonderful friends said I didn't have to pay rent for the first month. These acts of kindness and generosity might not seem like a huge deal, but they were life-changing for me.

As time passed, I got my feet anchored more securely under me. I asked myself, "What if God is on my side? What if He is actually helping me?" With a sincere desire to investigate, I got serious and got to work seeking answers to these questions.

CHAPTER 13
Freedom Isn't Free

RR

A FEW WEEKS INTO my journey to freedom, someone told me about a guy in Orange County, California, who had been sober longer than I had been alive. I was told this gentleman loved to take people through steps 1-8 of the Twelve Steps of the Alcoholics Anonymous (AA) program, and he would do it in an afternoon. I knew that the 12 steps were a sort of road map to recovery. "What did I have to lose?" I asked myself.

What a lot of people don't know, even some of those who have diligently followed the A.A. program for years, is that the Twelve Steps of AA were taken directly out of the Bible. William Griffith Wilson and Robert Smith were the co-founders of AA in 1935.

When describing the beginnings of AA, Bill W spoke of the significance of Reverend Samuel Moor Shoemaker III, a Princeton University graduate priest in the Episcopal Church. Shoemaker became one of the most powerful and influential speakers of his day. He was also head of the U.S. Oxford Group, a Christian organization dedicated to teaching each individual's need to "surrender one's life over to God's plan." (Wikipedia)

Reverend Shoemaker played a crucial role in Bill's recovery from alcoholism. After Bill attended his first Oxford Group meeting for drunks, he admitted himself for the fourth time to Towns Hospital, where he had a "spiritual experience" and never drank again after leaving the hospital. Bill W. later recalled the impact of first hearing Shoemaker preach of Christ, "It was a Sunday service in his church. I was still rather gun-shy and diffident about churches…Sam's utter honesty, his tremendous forthrightness, his almost terrible sincerity struck me deep. I shall never forget it." (Wikipedia)

Bill W. and Rev. Shoemaker became lifelong friends. As Bill W. described, "Dr. Sam Shoemaker was one of AA's indispensables. Had it not been for his ministry to us in our early time, our [AA] Fellowship would not be in existence today." Bill further noted, "It was from Sam Shoemaker that we absorbed most of the Twelve Steps of Alcoholics Anonymous, steps that express the heart of AA's way of life…He passed on the spiritual keys by which we were liberated." (Wikipedia)

A quick overview of the Twelve Steps in the AA program indicates their closeness to a biblical and simplified step-by-step confession and repentance process:

Step 1- We admitted we were powerless over alcohol—that our lives had become unmanageable.

Romans 7:18 For I know that nothing good lives within the flesh of my fallen humanity. The longings to do what is right are within me, but willpower is not enough to accomplish it. (TPT)

Step 2- Came to believe that a Power greater than ourselves could restore us to sanity.

Philippians 2:13 That energy is God's energy, an energy deep within you, God himself willing and working at what will give him the most pleasure. (Message Bible)

3. Made a decision to turn our will and our lives over to the care of God as we understood Him.

Romans 12:1 And so, dear brothers and sisters, I plead with you to give your bodies to God because of all he has done for you. Let them be a living and holy sacrifice—the kind he will find acceptable. This is truly the way to worship him. (NLT)

4. Made a searching and fearless moral inventory of ourselves.

Lamentations 3:40 Let us search out and examine our ways, And turn back to the LORD; (NKJV)

5. Admitted to God, to ourselves, and to another human being the exact nature of our wrongs.

James 5:16 Therefore, confess your sins to one another, and pray for one another so that you may be healed. A prayer of a righteous person, when it is brought about, can accomplish much. (NASB)

6. Were entirely ready to have God remove all these defects of character.

James 4:10 Be willing to be made low before the Lord and he will exalt you! (TPT)

7. Humbly asked Him to remove our shortcomings.

1 John 1:9, "If we confess our sins, he is faithful and will forgive us our sins and purify us from all unrighteousness." (NIV)

8. Made a list of all persons we had harmed, and became willing to make amends to them all.

Luke 6:31 Treat people the same way you want them to treat you. (NASB

9. Made direct amends to such people wherever possible, except when to do so would injure them or others.

Matthew 5:23-24, "This is how I want you to conduct yourself in these matters. If you enter your place of worship and, about to make an offering, you suddenly remember a grudge a friend has against you, 24 abandon your offering, leave immediately, go to this friend and make things right. Then and only then, come back and work things out with God. (Message Bible)

10. Continued to take personal inventory and when we were wrong promptly admitted it.

1 Corinthians 10:12 Therefore let the one who thinks he stands watch out that he does not fall. (NASB)

11. Sought through prayer and meditation to improve our conscious contact with God, as we understood Him, praying only for knowledge of His will for us and the power to carry that out.

Colossians 3:16 Let the word of Christ dwell in you richly, teaching and admonishing one another in all wisdom, singing psalms and hymns and spiritual songs, with thankfulness in your hearts to God. (ESV)

12. Having had a spiritual awakening as the result of these Steps, we tried to carry this message to alcoholics, and to practice these principles in all our affairs.

Galatians 6:1 Brothers and sisters, if someone is caught in a sin, you who live by the Spirit should restore that person gently. But watch yourselves, or you also may be tempted. (NIV)

A book written in 2008 by Dick B. called *"The James Club and the Original A. Program's Absolute Essentials"* clarifies the Christian roots of the AA program. It covers how early AA leaders frequently referenced the Book of James from the Bible, Jesus' Sermon on the Mount, and 1 Corinthians 13. These biblical passages were essential in A.A.'s early days. The Book of James was such an intricate piece to the early establishment of AA that they considered calling their group "The James Club."

I knew none of this as I drove north and found myself knocking on the door of a stranger to whom I had been recommended and to whom I was ready to disclose the secrets that had been keeping me sick for years. I didn't know what to expect, but I had been told that meeting with him would help keep me sober. Seeing as I couldn't stay sober on my own, I followed directions and made an appointment.

Moments after knocking, an old but alert gentleman opened the door and greeted me with a smile. He was a few inches shorter than I was, resting at just under six feet tall. His worn glasses, calm countenance, thin stature, and bald head eased a small portion of my anxiety. He said, "Hello, you must be Erik." After nodding my head, he announced that we would be "working" in his RV sitting in the driveway. This was the spiritual workshop where he would help me do the needed work to "clean up my side of the street."

John, we will call him, sat me down and explained that in the early days of A.A., they took people through the first eight steps of the Twelve Step program as quickly as possible. During those same early days, they also saw extremely high success rates for people stepping into the freedom of recovery. As he spoke, John's deep, focused eyes told stories in and of themselves. Just moments into our conversation, it was obvious that this man had survived the onslaught of hell and did not desire to return to that battlefield.

Also, as he began explaining the Twelve Steps to me, I knew he was not just "going through the motions." This was a man who took his part in the work of recovery seriously. I related to what he said as he laid out the recovery process and mixed it with stories from his days in addiction and early recovery. His journey was different from mine but the same. His stories had different details but the same outcomes.

I didn't know much about the Twelve Steps then, and I only grasped some of what he was conveying. But the bottom line was that I was ready to take orders. If John had lived through the hell he was talking about, and these steps were instrumental in setting him free from that hell, I was ready to follow those steps, too. I wanted and was ready to live free from my past and the patterns that kept leading me to hospitals, jails, rehabs, and thoughts of suicide.

When he spoke about the need to "confess my sins," I had some understanding of what he meant from my religious upbringing, and it made some sense to me. Embracing the moral obligation to take responsibility for my actions seemed like the least I should do after all the destruction I'd left in my wake. This part of the Twelve Step process seemed in line with what those in my situation needed to do.

Another big reason I was willing to embark on the Twelve Step journey was that I had sat in recovery meetings and listened to people share their stories. I'd hear the similarities of my story in their story. I heard them talk about not wanting to keep drinking and using drugs but having no power over the spiritual curse of addiction. I felt the same way.

It was easy to find myself in their stories. I also heard how they did the Twelve Steps and how it helped them transform their lives. So, I thought to myself, "If these weirdos can stay sober, anyone can." It was a funny assessment, considering where I'd been and what others may have said about me.

So, there I was with some old guy, sitting in his driveway in his RV, ready to take directions from him and, more amazingly, expose the secrets of my life to him. First things first, he gave me a big bag of M&M's, Mountain Dew, and a pen and paper—my kind of guy!

I was already at steps four and five by this point in my journey. The first three steps were about surrender and believing that God could and would change me, and I was already on page with that. After talking with John, my new old friend, about those first three steps for a few minutes, he could tell I was also ready for steps four and five. As stated above, these steps require the individual to:

4. Made a searching and fearless moral inventory of ourselves and

5. Admit to God, to ourselves, and to another human being the exact nature of our wrongs.

I thought then, "That doesn't seem too hard." With pen and paper in my hand, he explained that I needed to do this as simply and fully as possible. He then got up, told me he would return in an hour, and went into his house. *"If this worked for countless others, it should work for me,"* I thought to myself, and I got to work writing out on paper as many wrongdoings as my mind could recollect.

I wrote down everything I could think of. I was prepared to "Admit to God, to ourselves and to another human being the exact nature of our wrongs." (Step 5, James 5:16)

It was extraordinary that at this point in my journey, my understanding and experience of Christ, His power, and His forgiveness began to clarify itself as a reality in my life. I began to connect the dots. For me to be free from my past wrongdoings, someone had to pay the penalties. Ultimately, the judge of all mankind had to render a decision that my debt had been paid, and therefore, I was freed from the consequences of my actions. I have experienced this process many times in the natural world. However, I would now begin to experience it in spirit and soul while sitting in old John's RV in Orange County, California.

All my past sins were still legally hanging over my head. The enemy still had legal rights over me because I had committed these wrongdoings. Although Christ had paid the penalty, I had not done my due diligence and gone through the correct process of repenting to receive Christ's free gift of forgiveness.

In the same way that a police officer was within his legal rights to arrest me for past and present crimes I had committed, for which I had not paid the consequences, the devil still had power over me. He still had the power to shape and control my thoughts and to torment me to the point I often felt like I was a puppet on a string. I was a slave to demonic forces. The dark spiritual reality had invisible chains wrapped around me.

In Colossians 2, the Apostle Paul describes it this way, "When you were stuck in your old sin-dead life, you were incapable of responding to God. God brought you alive—right along with Christ! Think of it! All sins forgiven, the slate wiped clean, that old arrest warrant canceled and nailed to Christ's cross." (Message Bible) Christ's victory on the cross gives us victory in the present, over our past, and in the future. His sacrifice on the cross paid in full the price for the sins of the world, and in doing so, as we repent and receive forgiveness, He strips any and all authority over us away from the powers of darkness.

Months prior, in that little courtroom in Utah, God showed me He was wiping my slate clean in the court of law. He was also drawing me into a relationship with His perfect Son, who would also erase the legal consequences of my spiritual misdeeds.

This remarkable privilege now lay before me: to take responsibility for my wrongdoings, admit them to God and man, and do it humbly and honestly. I sat in that old, comfortable RV with pen and paper and wrote everything that came to mind. I thought, *I'm leaving nothing out.* The worst memories of past actions I planned on taking to the grave were the first things I wrote down.

I wrote down my wrongdoings, taking ownership of my actions— and my actions only--, as I gobbled M&M's and guzzled Mountain Dew. Before I knew it, I had five pages written down. Seeing it on paper sparked me to say to myself, "Wow, I was a real idiot."

This step in the process was my personal freedom thesis. I declared I had broken God's laws and, in so doing, distanced myself from Him and His love. I agreed that I needed to be saved from the consequences of my actions and that I did not have the power in and of myself to do this. I willingly exposed my darkness so "the Light of the world" would fill me with the light of His presence.

I had always gone pedal to the metal in my addiction. I figured I'd try that in recovery as well. Attempting to be fully honest with God was the course I needed to pursue. As Mark Twain's character, Tom Sawyer, once explained, "You can't pray a lie," meaning you can't deceive God.

God sees you. He knows you. He knows if your heart is in the right place. He knows if you are genuinely sorry for what you have done.

There I was with caffeine, sugar, and the hope of freedom coursing through my blood. When I finished, I went and knocked on his garage door. He opened and smiled and followed me back to his RV.

He sat ready to listen as I puked my past all over him. He remained calm, unfazed. When I finished, he said, "That's it?" He then told me some of the worst things he had done. I think he did this to ease my nerves and let me know that we were in this together.

I thought to myself, "Wow. This guy has issues."

We went through some more work, and we prayed together. He then sent me on my way and told me to keep doing the work daily. I remember making the forty-five-minute drive back to Oceanside that day and noticing something was different. I did not experience a dramatic moment of Divine manifestation, but I clearly remember feeling lighter. "Something" had been lifted off me. It was like I had been carrying a big backpack full of heavy rocks when I knocked on John's door. I knew the discomfort of this weight; I had been carrying it for years. Upon departing and driving home, that weight was strangely unpresent.

Christ promised in *Matthew 11: 28-30, "Come to Me, all who are weary and burdened, and I will give you rest. Take My yoke upon you and learn from Me, for I am gentle and humble in heart, and you will find rest for your souls. For My yoke is comfortable, and My burden is light."* *(NASB)*

CHAPTER 14
A Whole New World

RR

Amy "thesis of freedom," a new freedom began to take up residence in me. I noticed it without fully understanding the beauty and depth of what had truly taken place. I began to sense a foreign spiritual presence growing inside me; it was new and filled me with wonder.

I had wished, hoped, and prayed desperate prayers during my years of addiction, desperate for the new freedom I was finally beginning to taste. However, I had never met freedom and didn't know what freedom really looked or felt like. I had seen other people live in what I perceived as freedom, as they smiled and lived productive lives, but having never lived in it, I didn't yet fully know how to identify it in my emerging world.

If someone had asked me to define freedom up until that point of my life, I would have said something along the lines of, "I am free to do what I want, when I want." But strangely, that mentality kept landing me in places that robbed me of my freedom.

Freedom was an interesting new experience for me as I allowed it to slowly tiptoe into my world. It was like a pretty lady walking up to me, holding out her hand and saying, "Would you like to dance?" "Ah, sure, but just for your information, I don't know how to dance the way you're dancing."

I knew all too well how to dance to the rhythm of fear, constant worry, shame, and guilt. But I didn't know how to move to the rhythm of peace, joy, clarity, and honesty. As fear-filled realities began to vacate my life, it felt like breaking up with a bad girlfriend. I had grown so accustomed to having dark and weighty clouds follow me that it almost felt irresponsible, in a strange way, when they left.

I can still recall the newness when peace, joy, and self-control began to take hold in my life, and I would stop and think, "Not sure if I deserve this. Shouldn't I be worrying about something?" Clearly, I needed to upgrade my thinking surrounding what truly was freedom. So, I prayed, studied, and dug deeper into understanding what freedom is because it's certainly not what so many voices in today's world teach us it is.

First, I had to understand and recognize the difference between free will and freedom. I (or you) can indeed do whatever I want whenever I want, albeit with consequences, some good, others bad. This type of "doing what I want, when I want" is defined as free will, but it is not freedom. I had abused my free will for much of my life. I used my free will to try and feel good, or what I thought felt good, until a certain point in my life. But doing so kept landing me in jails, rehabs, hospitals, horrible relationships, and so on.

Sadly, in many ways, we are socialized in today's world through movies, TV, music, books, peer pressure, social media, etc., to do what we want when we want, believing there are no adverse consequences, and it shows. Without knowing it, I was fed widespread lies and embraced them to conform to the patterns of this world. For example, I watched movies that normalized and encouraged young people to party, party, party! If that's not bad enough, those same movies rarely showed the horrors of addiction or other poor choices.

It is hard to "step outside the box" and see the lies and falsehoods in what we are encouraged and socialized to do. Even more tragic, young people with little real-world experience against which to judge these behaviors are subtly socialized, easily manipulated, and deceived into engaging in dangerous, self-destructive activities.

But at this point in my early journey with God, I was learning step-by-step how to change my behavior. One of the first things that dawned on me was that the lie of addiction always promised what only God could deliver.

"You are *free* to party tonight," would be the lie broadcasting inside my mind. I'd join that conversation with the enemy and reply, "Yeah, that's right! I am *free* to do what I want." Then I'd drink myself into a blackout and often get in trouble. My idea of doing what I wanted because "I'm *free* to do what I want" never gave me freedom—it only took it away.

The demons accompanying addiction would whisper into my mind and heart, telling me that drugs and alcohol would make me more creative, give me more energy, help me have more fun, make me smarter, and the list goes on. However, addiction was the enemy. It gave me the exact opposite of what it promised. It took me into the most hellish Haunted House and terrorized me for years until God's grace invaded my life.

My adventure into this new world required me to learn a new culture and language. And the fastest way to learn a new language is to immerse yourself in it. It is vital to study it, understand the phonetics, and know the culture of those who speak the language.

I recognized something new was going on when I suddenly had money in my pocket and could walk in and out of a store without being tempted to buy alcohol. Soon, that became my new normal. Most people cannot understand this unless they have dragged the ball and chain of addiction and its demonic culture around like a portable prison for years.

I saw evidence of growth when I could control my responses and stop associating with "friends" that I knew would prevent me from walking into my destiny and true identity. I began to realize a new culture of freedom was taking root when I realized it was as easy, if not easier, to get marijuana in Southern California than it was to get alcohol, yet I had the self-control to refrain. Addiction never delivered freedom because its promises were false. But God was delivering on His promise of freedom in my life as I partnered with Him. Walking with Jesus allowed me to begin to know real fun and to feel good, mentally and physically. I embarked on a journey, and my new leader was God Himself.

I was beginning to taste real freedom, and that sweet taste made me want to know more about the teachings of the One that granted me freedom.

I believe that is why the Bible says, "Taste and see that the Lord is good." (Psalm 34:8). I began waking up early and reading His Word. Then, as I journaled and prayed, I began to see obvious positive changes in my thinking and perspective on life.

For years, my diet in the temporal realm was complete garbage, with both the food and content I consumed. I didn't fully understand that what I ingested into my belly and brain played a big part in how I saw the world. Think about how our chemistry, as well as our perspective, immediately changes if we eat sugar or drink caffeine. We could list everything we eat and drink and their effect on our brains and bodies. Some of the substances we consume bring an immediate effect, and all of them affect our long-term health and perspective.

It began to make sense that if I filled myself with God's presence, His reality would be reflected in my thoughts and actions. Just as what we physically eat plays a huge role in how we think, act, and speak, God helped me see the need to begin each day with a spiritual meal prepared by God. So that's what I did. I got up early, and spiritually speaking, I ate a big healthy meal as I feasted on God and His Word.

There is something freeing about individual quiet time early in the morning. To this day, every day, I'm up before the sun rises. I sit at my kitchen table with my Bible and journal and start with prayer. I am writing this at 4 a.m., in the quiet, with God. It's a discipline that produces glorious rewards.

Early in my recovery journey, I began going to bed early because I was excited to get up early and spend time with God. In my first year of recovery, I would wake up, roll off the small, single mattress I slept on, just a few inches off the ground, and relish in the silence and peace I felt. The National Library of Medicine cited a 2006 study by Stice, Burton, Bearman, & Rohde. Their results showed that daily journaling produced "significantly greater reductions in depressive symptoms." It also indicated that daily journaling can be as beneficial as therapy in lessening the risks of depression.

I immediately began to recognize that writing was beneficial. The more I wrote about things I was pondering and described how and why I was thinking those thoughts, the more clarity I experienced.

If my mind was going fast or lies were bouncing around in my brain like a pinball game, I'd pray and write, and my mind would slow down. My perspective would change, and I'd almost immediately be able to see things in a more hope-filled way. Later, I learned that people who write regularly experience better sleep, better memory recall, and lower blood pressure, just to name a few health benefits.

With only a lamp, some books, and my hungry heart, God would meet me. He certainly wasn't impressed with my knowledge; I didn't have much in the way of knowledge at that time. And he certainly didn't care about my makeshift setup. But He knew about the posture of my heart, and He responded to that. I knew next to nothing about God, but by this time, I knew He was on my side and that my life depended on knowing Him. And not just knowing about Him, I had to know Him personally.

When I journaled, I wrote about what I was thinking and what questions went through my mind as I read through the Bible and AA books. I'd pray about what I wrote in my journal and sit and soak up the peace that entered my room. No one told me what to do or how to do this morning routine, and I had no theological explanation for what was happening. All I knew was that it was working.

I was now the captain of my ship, and this was my time to study the maps and prepare myself for whatever the storms of life would throw at me. I found that the more time I spent each morning with God, the more I could avoid stormy seas and find still and peaceful waters.

This slow but steady daily transformation in my life was new and challenging. Growing up, I had formulated the idea that to do things like pray, read the Bible, and learn about God, I had to be perfect. So, it caught me off-guard when I started hearing God and experiencing Him in my life--while being anything but perfect.

I still smoked cigarettes. I still cussed like a sailor. I still had a pornography addiction and was still having sex outside of marriage.

The residue of thirteen years of living like a hellion didn't leave me overnight--but it was leaving. That was for sure. Drugs and alcohol were gone from my life, and self-control rose within me daily.

I never looked at my morning routine as if it was a religious "to-do list." I simply looked at it as a great time spent with my Dad in Heaven. Having a relationship with God was talked about frequently in A.A., so I just tried to have a relationship with Him as best I could.

At times, my morning routine felt robotic, but I knew it helped me stay sober and grow in maturity and my relationship with God. I followed my time with God every morning by attending a 7 a.m. AA meeting with Darin and Eileen.

The amazing thing about this specific meeting was that it was three or four minutes from where we lived, and it was a smaller meeting of mostly older people. Not only were they older, but most people there had at least ten years of recovery, if not twenty years. It was a gift.

I recollect the first time I walked into this meeting. My new roommates had invited me to join them for this early morning meet-up the previous night. Knowing that I needed this in my life, I agreed to take this uncomfortable step simply for the sake of gaining more comfort.

Up early the following day, I was ready to go a few minutes before departure time. We hopped in Darin's SUV and made the short drive to a church. Not knowing what to expect, my heart rate escalated as we entered the parking lot. I exited the car and walked towards the meeting room, anxiously anticipating the unexpected. We made our way down the pathway behind the main sanctuary toward a smaller building. As we walked into this rectangular space centered by a long rectangular table. I noticed some smiling old ladies shaking hands and chatting. Their warm smiles lessened my anxiety a bit.

Half of the group were men. They were congregating and laughing. I remember asking myself, "What are these people laughing about? This can't be all fun and games."

One older lady, maybe 5' 2', one hundred pounds, came up to welcome me. She introduced herself with a recognizable sense of peace and confidence. "What does she want?" I wondered to myself as I smiled and shook her hand. Moments later, this meeting of roughly 20 people was called to order.

Everyone sat calmly, exuding a certain seriousness. I observed. I listened, and strangely, I felt accepted. They did not want anything from me-- this was new. I sat and listened to people who had really been through the wringer of addiction as they talked freely about the past and the present. They spoke about the process they went through and shared about coming to know God and stewarding His freedom in their lives. My heart rate skipped whenever someone finished sharing because I thought I might have to say something next.

These people were not intimidating, but the open and honest environment was intimidating. It led to a conversation in my head, "These people all know what they're talking about. If I have to say something in here, they will clearly know that I know nothing about this recovery thing." Then the moment came, and the tiny, sweet older woman who greeted me as I walked in called on me and asked if I would like to share something.

My heart rate revved, like someone pressing the gas pedal on a car still in park. I said, "Sure," trying to mask my nervousness. I didn't share for long and certainly didn't share anything revelatory with this group, but they listened. I knew they genuinely cared, and I felt no judgment. Without fully realizing it, I was experiencing the culture behind this new foreign language and this reality called freedom.

I was immersed in a culture of acceptance. They accepted me for who I was. They appreciated where I was on my journey. As a matter of fact, they wanted to hear from me because it reminded them of their earlier steps on the path to recovery. I made some friends. Oddly, these were not people I would have chosen as friends. We were misfits of all ages, races, backgrounds, and experiences, but we had one thing in common. We all wanted to know God and to live in the land of freedom for another day.

I was there bright and early, at 7 a.m., Monday through Friday, for nearly a year after that. I made dear, treasured friends there. I asked questions. I learned to listen and slowly learned more about God in that little musky room that always smelled of stale coffee.

CHAPTER 15
Living Loved

RR

HAVE YOU EVER had a moment when you looked in the mirror and didn't know who you were looking at? I mean, I knew what I looked like. I knew my name, my family, and what I had experienced and been taught until that point in my life. But the truth is, I did not know my identity. I did not know my purpose. I did not know what I was supposed to do with my life.

I was at a place where it was literally time to reinvent myself. But what was reinventing myself going to look like? Until now, I hadn't given much thought to the notion, "Who am I? What is my identity?"

I was beginning to expect some good things in my life, and I increasingly believed it was possible to have a promising future. God had come into my life. He had forgiven me and welcomed me and my curiosity with open, loving arms as my journey of freedom began. It was as if I was being resurrected from the dead. I was slowly transitioning from spiritual infancy and awkwardly moving into a spiritual standing toddler. My new lease on life pushed me into a genuine search to find out, "Who am I, and what's my purpose?"

It may be one of the most important questions we should ask. Think about the fact that when we get down to the nitty-gritty, no two of us are alike. Estimates indicate that 105 billion people have lived on planet Earth, and of those 105 billion people, no two people have ever had the same fingerprint. Since 1892, when Juan Vucetich, an Argentinian Chief of Police, began recording fingerprints of individuals, no one has ever found two identical fingerprints.

Consider also facial recognition software. I gain access to my iPhone only after it scans my face and confirms a match to the scan stored on my phone. The website CSIS.ORG describes, "In ideal conditions, facial recognition systems can have near-perfect accuracy...99.97% on standard assessments...Face verification has become so reliable that even banks feel comfortable logging users into their accounts."

I struggled to understand my identity most of my life. In the confusion created by our social media-driven world, it's easy to fall into the trap of trying to find yourself by trying to be like someone else or constantly comparing yourself to others. Pastor Steven Furtick of the Elevation Church said it best when he explained, "The reason we struggle with insecurity is because we compare our behind-the-scenes with everyone else's highlight reel." It's not fair or right to compare ourselves to others to understand who we are. I wasn't created to be you, and you weren't created to be me. We are all wonderfully different!

I heard people who had been in the A.A. fellowship for an extended period of time say things like, "You're not unique. You're not different from the rest of us." But this is a situation where those words have a different connotation. In an A.A. meeting, those words are intended to convey to the "newcomer" that they aren't different in their struggle with addiction than the person next to them.

Those words are spoken because alcoholics often try to plead their case as to why they are different when it comes to their drinking problem when, in reality, they are just desperately trying to rationalize their drinking. They engage in "stinkin' thinkin'" to try and excuse their never-ending drinking. "You're an alcoholic. You're not any different than any of us. Sit down and learn some things," was the message to the newcomer. It was a powerful and much-needed message for the person coming out of the fog of addiction. It's meant to confront the bad habit of making excuses that keep the alcoholic drinking. "I don't really have a problem. I just had a bad few months," or, "My life is really hard. Drinking helps me cope," and the list goes on.

Yet, while we share similarities in certain aspects of human living, the truth of our identity is that each of us is unique and distinct. Science and technology affirm that there is no one on the planet like me or you. My eyes began to open wider as God started showing me that I am "fearfully and wonderfully made," as King David pointed out in Psalm 139. The truth of this is enhanced by a more detailed definition of "wonderfully made." From the original Hebrew, you find the word *palah*. It means separate or distinct. God made each of us an original masterpiece of His creative expression. You and I are an original creation created in *His image and likeness*. We are not copies of someone else.

As I began to reflect on my life, I realized I had long been on an unrecognized, unfulfilled quest to find out who I was going as far back as I could remember. I was pushed into trying to find my identity in religion at a young age. I hated it. I attempted to find my identity through sports and athletic performance. That never fully satisfied me. I was relentless in trying to find myself through drugs and alcohol. That made my life a living hell. I tried through music, but that wasn't fulfilling for me. I tried through hollow relationships and by regularly swapping out girlfriends. I could never find true fulfillment and satisfaction, not where I was looking.

I was trying to find my life and identity in everything I did rather than turning to the Source of Life Himself. For years, I periodically wondered why I was here on Earth. Why was I created? For what purpose was I created? Sober and clearer-minded, I now began to realize that God created me as an original expression of His love. I had been looking in all the wrong places for years when I should have been asking The One who created me.

I began seeking answers from my Creator, and the most important answer I received was to the question, "Who am I?"

It sounded sappy and weird to think about or seek answers to these age-old questions, "Who am I?" And, "What is love?" Yet, while it is possibly the most important question a person should seek to know, I'd never really spent time and effort contemplating these questions.

Consequently, my life up until that time was a direct result of not knowing I was a beloved child of God.

How many books, poems, movies, magazines, and music have tried to convey who we are and what love is? How often are we misinformed and led down a rabbit hole? How many individuals actually know they are God's child, created and loved by Him? I suppose I might have defined love as a good emotional feeling of some sort towards someone. My definition of love was based on how I was feeling that day. One day, I may have said I loved life because things were going well. The next day, I might have said I hated life because I wasn't feeling good. This emotional roller coaster demonstrated my cluelessness and why I floundered for so long.

My identity was based on who others wanted me to be or the often unachievable perfectionist standard I held myself to. I only loved others or treated them according to what my definition of love was that day--according to what they could do for me or had done for me.

I was clueless that love is perfectly defined in the Bible. Love is who God is and why He does what He does. As defined in 1 Corinthians 13:4-5, "Love is patient, love is kind, it is not jealous; love does not brag and is not arrogant, does not act unbecomingly." (NASB) I had already been experiencing this, but my next experience with Love would mark me forever. And while I thought it would take God Himself screaming into a megaphone inches from my ear to start understanding love, instead, it was a whisper in my ear.

It was my first Christmas in recovery, and my sister (the same sister that God used to save my life when I tried to kill myself) and her husband invited me to come out to Flagstaff, Arizona, and spend a few days with them. I was excited to go, but there was one problem. I was broke. I knew if I went, I likely wouldn't have enough money for gas to make it back to San Diego. I did the only thing I now knew to do to get the right answer: I prayed. What followed was amazing.

I was on my knees the following morning, well before the sun rose. As my little lamp lit the room, I prayed and laid out my requests and concerns about traveling to be with my sister and her family for Christmas.

As I asked God if I should go and, if so, how to make it work, I heard an audible voice whisper to me, "Don't worry about it. I'll take care of it." The voice was soft yet firm, as if someone leaned close to tell me a secret an inch from my ear. I literally felt the breath on the words as they whispered and echoed down my ear canal. It startled me.

I opened my eyes wide, knowing full well no one was in the room—but Someone was. This was new. I felt like I'd heard God speak to me before as He put thoughts in my mind. I also knew He spoke to me through other people or through experiences, but this was the first time I heard an audible voice so close I could feel the breath on the words.

God was extending an invitation for me to follow Him. He wanted to take me on a journey of trust and love. Second Corinthians 4:18 teaches, "So we don't look at the troubles we can see now; rather, we fix our gaze on things that cannot be seen. For the things we see now will soon be gone, but the things we cannot see will last forever." I was learning I was uniquely created in love to be in continual connection to Jesus Christ who was Love personified. Yet, I had difficulty taking my eyes off the troubles before me. In many ways, the filter for my future was still dialed into the experience of my past. I was still having trouble fixing my vision on my Provider. His firm, invisible whisper of Love was to remind me that He was my Provider.

Let's pause for a moment. When someone says something like, "I heard a voice," nowadays, it might cause listeners to raise a curious eyebrow. The truth is, however, every single one of us hears voices. Think about it. Where do you think all your thoughts are coming from? When you have random good thoughts, aren't you "hearing" something in your mind?

When I say we all hear voices, I'm not talking about hearing audible voices that scream crazy things in our ears and tell us to do things that hurt us or others. These dark, tormenting realities and mental health disorders are very real. I'm talking about the roughly 60,000 thoughts a day the average person experiences. We do hear things in our heads. I never gave this reality a second thought. I never looked at it like I was hearing things in my mind. Most of the time, I just went with whatever thought popped into my head.

Now, here I was, twenty-seven years old, passionately and intentionally seeking God daily. And suddenly, a clear, unmistakable voice says, "Don't worry about it, I'll take care of it." I must admit, I didn't tell anyone about it because I didn't think anyone would believe me, but I knew that what I heard and experienced was similar to the half dozen or so times the Holy Spirit came and cooked me in His fiery presence when I was a young and confused teenager. I didn't want to tell anyone about those supernatural encounters at that time, either. So, what did I do? I left a few days later and drove to Flagstaff, Arizona, with only an audible promise from God that He would take care of my needs. I made the seven-and-a-half-hour drive and arrived to enjoy a sober Christmas Eve with my sister, her husband, and their two kids.

Christmas morning arrived, and I can honestly say that I didn't expect much. Just the invitation was a great kindness. I didn't know what would happen, and I was just trying not to worry about how I'd pay for the drive home. After waking to celebrate the birth of King Jesus, I watched everyone open presents. My niece and nephew did so with expectant smiles and outbursts of joy, and I was able to soak it all in. Then we ate a great Christmas meal. It was wonderful to be with my family and to be present on Christmas Day.

Then it happened. After we ate, my sister took me aside and said, "Oh yeah, we got something for you." Deep down, I suppose I was hoping for something, even though I had nothing to give that day. She took me into the room I was sleeping in, and next to my bed was a small Christmas tree, maybe three feet tall. My brother-in-law had put it in my room when I was out in the living room watching everyone open presents.

Pinned all over the tree was money: ten-dollar bills, twenty-dollar bills, five-dollar bills, and one-dollar bills were clipped to the branches of the tree--over one hundred and sixty dollars in total. Time stood still as my eyes watered, and I instantly recalled the moment when Love Himself broke into my world with an invisible whisper telling me to go be with my family and that He would take care of me.

What could I even do? I thanked my sister and my brother-in-law and sat speechless for some time. I couldn't fully grasp the magnitude of what happened that Christmas morning. It was years later that I fully unwrapped that gift.

My whole life, I hadn't thought much about, or paid attention to, who and what I was. I was God's beloved child. I got into trouble because I ignored this great truth and sought my identity in all the wrong ways and all the wrong places. My journey into my identity had begun, but I still had little understanding of who I was. But God started by driving home that His love for me was unconditional and His goodness was unending. Before I went about trying to fulfill my purpose, He wanted me to know that I was loved.

I didn't deserve all the grace He was showering on me. He'd wiped my slate clean in the court of law. I experienced His forgiveness. He gave me a place to live with individuals who mentored me. He surrounded me with good people, and when I needed to learn more about trusting Him in my life, He provided me with the money to travel and be with my sister and her family at Christmas. We learn more about his matchless love when we consider his supreme gift to us in John 3:16, "*For God so loved the world, that He gave His only begotten Son, that whoever believes in Him shall not perish, but have eternal life.*" This leads us also to ask, what is eternal life? Well, for starters, it is not of this world. It is from above, and it began growing in me when I said "Yes" to Jesus.

As I began to embrace this relationship with God, I began to live out eternal life, "*And this is eternal life, that they may know You, the only true God, and Jesus Christ whom You have sent,*" as the Apostle of Love, John, wrote in chapter seventeen of The Gospel of John. The experience of eternal life started when I began pursuing a relationship with Jesus.

On the day of celebrating the birth of the visible image of love, Jesus Christ, I should have been giving gifts away, but I couldn't because I didn't have the resources to do so. Yet that didn't stop God from freely giving to me in ways to meet both my temporal and, more importantly, my spiritual hunger.

Maybe I did give Him a gift that day. Perhaps the fact that I trusted Him a little bit was my gift to Him. At Christmas, He gave me a gift far beyond the wonderful money tree I received. He gave me the gift of knowing who I am in His eyes: a loved and cherished child of God.

CHAPTER 16
The Renewing of the Mind

RR

THE STRANGE YET exhilarating part about any journey into unknown land is that every single step is a step into uncharted territory. Once I left the land of the walking dead and entered the land of the living, all forward motion was a new experience on new terrain. At times, this was a bit frightening because a commitment to a new adventure is a commitment to the unknown.

I quickly learned that one of the biggest keys to navigating this new land of hope and opportunity was learning how to leave the unhealthy patterns and habits of the past. I also learned that they would repeat themselves if my unhealthy patterns were not addressed and corrected.

In April 2021, The Bureau of Justice Statistics (BJS) released a report called "Recidivism of Prisoners Released in 34 States in 2012: A 5-Year Follow-Up Period (2012–2017)." Here are a few highlights from their findings:

-Almost 6 in 10 (62%) of the prisoners released across 34 states in 2012 were arrested for and charged with crimes within 3 years, and 7 in 10 (71%) were arrested within 5 years.

-Eighty-one percent of prisoners age 24 or younger, released in 2012, were arrested after committing crimes within 5 years of release, compared to 74% of those ages 25 to 39, and 61% of those age 40 or older.

-Nearly half (46%) of the prisoners released in 2012 returned to prison within 5 years for a parole or probation violation, or after being convicted of another crime.

The parallel and the irony here is that each time I got a new start or left rehab, I, too, had a chance to start a new life. So why did so much insanity continue to play out in my life all those years? For starters, just because someone is released from a physical prison doesn't mean they are released from the spiritual, emotional, and mental prison in which they live. Although many reasons factor into this situation, understanding our brains and minds and how they function will help us understand what a person needs to do if they hope to effect real change in their life.

Besides the need to understand and sort out our thinking on this matter, another element must be considered. That is the spiritual battle that the individual must fight. And the enemy that confronts us does not want you or me to step into the freedom God has made available to His children.

I recall experiencing some of this supernatural resistance in a real way during the early stages of my spiritual transformation. It occurred early in recovery when I was attending A.A. meetings daily. At the end of many meetings, those attending will "circle up" and hold hands and pray "The Serenity Prayer" or "The Lord's Prayer" in unison. One particularly disquieting experience occurred at a meeting I was attending for the first time. As we wrapped up our encouraging meeting, we circled, grasped each other's hands, and began praying. I was feeling good and strengthened. But as we started "Our Father," I was immediately hit with what I now know was spiritual warfare, stiff resistance from the devil in the form of the lingering memories and tempting lies associated with addiction.

As the words rolled off my lips, my mind began playing and looping movie reels of getting drunk. The images were so clear that a hologram was playing out in front of me on the old wooden flooring of an upstairs room in an old bar. "Who art in Heaven," we continued in unison, as old memories pushed their way to the forefront of my imagination with so much clarity it was as if I was reliving the moment. Past experiences where I might have had a moment of fun, as well as memories of dark depression, a car wreck, someone dying, and the list goes on.

"Hallowed be thy name," we kept praying as new movie reels played wild scenes on the canvas of my mind. I was the main character, yet I was an audience member watching forbidden yet hauntingly tempting scenes play out in my mind. Clearly, this enemy was confronting me and attempting to impede my positive forward progress at the exact moment I was doing everything I could to strengthen my relationship with God. This conflict between good and evil continued as we prayed.

After the prayer ended, I did my best to act as if nothing had happened, certain I was the only one having this experience. Through it all, though, I kept wondering, "What in the world is happening?" all the while experiencing episodes of reliving past experiences. I had no answer to that question at that time.

But over the years, as I pondered and learned, I came to understand what was happening. Vestiges of lingering darkness remained in my consciousness, and the enemy behind that hideous darkness was desperate to maintain and reignite his power over me at the same moment I was being invigorated by the Light and Power of God and His kingdom. Like an angry, petulant child in complete meltdown, the master of darkness kicked and screamed because he didn't want to lose me.

Those intense moments during group AA prayers continued for a season. I kept those spiritual contests to myself. I didn't want people to think I was crazy, and I didn't know who to talk to about these matters because, up until that point, I had never heard anyone talk about anything like this. I did not understand that every day, the lingering darkness in my life was getting closer and closer to being evicted. Light and darkness were on a collision course; my mind, body, and soul were the battlegrounds where this conflict played out.

Looking back now, I realize that God countered the darkness at every turn as He fueled me with His grace, and He hasn't stopped doing so since I began partnering with Him. God was the reason I could push past and prevail in this almost military-like contest to further my spiritual growth. As I kept my eyes on and trusted God, relying on Him daily, studying his Word, praying, and doing as much good as possible, my opponent weakened and finally departed. Don't misunderstand. The enemy doesn't give up. He is no match for the King of Kings, and as we fix our gaze on the Author and Finisher of our faith, the enemy must waddle off like a defeated mutt with his tail between his legs.

Another interesting research study that is pertinent here was conducted in 2005 by the National Science Foundation. When they published their findings on research centered on human thought life, they found that the average person has as many as 60,000 thoughts in a single day. They also found that around eighty percent of those thoughts are negative. Further, about ninety-five percent of those thoughts were on repeat from the previous day.

Their research indicated that most of our thought patterns are negative and loop over and over through our minds daily. And this makes perfect sense because, in far too many ways, we live in an inherently negative world. We can't get very far into a day without seeing or hearing something negative in nature.

Let's consider one example of this. When did you last watch the news and come away feeling encouraged or hopeful? Think as well about the music to which we listen. How much of its content promotes positive, hope-filled thoughts? The same question can be asked with regard to TV shows, movies, magazines, billboards, books, conversations we engage in or overhear, etc. Up until I began extricating myself from addictive thinking and practices, I let the enemy hit me like a punching bag because I did not understand that so many of our mental and spiritual battles are lost because of the thoughts we entertain in our minds.

I grew up listening to rap music. As anyone who listens to rap music knows, it overwhelmingly and persistently promotes sex, drugs, drinking, and violence. The inevitable byproduct of filling my mind with this spiritual garbage was that these practices became a reality in my life. The results will be the same if the movies, TV shows, and streaming services we watch promote these practices. If the books, magazines, online content we read, the conversations we have, and the people with whom we surround ourselves spew negativity, odds are we will also embrace these practices.

Before I escaped the fog, I was essentially clueless that the enemy himself was using all the above to plant and water seeds of darkness in my mind. The intense flashbacks I had while praying with a group at the end of A.A. meetings were meant to sow again the dark seeds planted in my psyche years earlier.

Additional scientific research backs up the premise that the way we think not only plays a critical role in our actions but does so because it changes the physical structure of our brains. Scientists call this Neural Plasticity. A 1949 scientific study led by Donald Hebb discovered that "neurons that fire together wire together."

What does this mean? Our brain is made up of roughly 100 billion neurons with approximately 100 trillion neural connections, or pathways, along which a thought can travel to its destination. When a thought enters our mind, our neurons fire up and establish a new Neural Pathway. When another thought comes to our mind that agrees or connects with a previously generated thought, and as more do so over time, they slowly but surely establish well-used Neural Pathways. This process starts in the mind, then carves its paths in the brain, and then plays out through our words and actions. Once thinking patterns are established, it takes understanding and intentionality to re-route or change our thinking.

In my addiction-laced life, years and years of unhealthy, destructive thinking dug deep, destructive "thought highways" into my brain. I had work to do to change my life and repurpose it for good. I needed to establish healthy, positive thought highways through my mind. I needed to create a new psychological infrastructure and establish new neural pathways that led me to glorious outcomes and desirable destinations. The Good News, the great news, is that God can and will cleanse and renew our minds as we seek His help. He can and will heal our brains, and He will clear a magnificent path for us that will take us to the heights of glory and unimagined beauty as we follow Him.

Over the last eleven-plus years, I've had the privilege of talking or working with thousands of people. Sometimes, we engaged in a simple conversation or a series of conversations, followed by prayer.

Sometimes, conversations occurred during the countless coaching sessions I have conducted with clients in my Life and Sober Coaching practice. During these many conversations, I have heard about horrific upbringings experienced by many individuals—truly crushing, heart-breaking stories. I also worked with many individuals who grew up being taught by good, caring parents and family members but made a bad choice, or two or more, that eventually led them down a dark road where they stumbled and wandered for years.

I have met endless people who were written off to a life of problems and pain because they burned all their bridges and destroyed everything good. Yet I've seen those same people, time and time again, partner with God and turn their lives around. They changed in such dramatic ways that if you had not known them before their transformation, you would never in a million years think they previously lived in chaos and misery.

No matter how low someone has gone in their attempt to dig their way to "rock bottom," one thing we can know for sure is that over thousands of years, a wealth of evidence from millions of individual's lives testifies that God loves to take the worst of the worst and power-fully transform their lives as He uses them for His glory. He can change dark thinking. He can transform us from the inside out. He can lead us out of destructive behaviors, help us establish new neural pathways, and find joy as we go about doing good in the world.

In the New Testament, in Romans 12:2, the Apostle Paul writes about how God can and will renew our minds, *"And do not be conformed to this world, but be transformed by the renewing of your mind, that you may prove what is that good and acceptable and perfect will of God."* (NKJV)

Two driving factors enabled me to tear down my confused mind and begin renewing and rebuilding it with God. First, I began the practice of speaking to Him daily in prayer. Second, I feasted on God's words. I began by sitting daily in my little room, with my little lamp and Bible, seeking Him as I prayed and thought through what I read. My ways of thinking from the past had led me into darkness and chaos. It was imperative I vacate those old pathways, clear and construct new pathways, and, in doing so, establish a new, thriving, vibrant psychological and spiritual infrastructure in my mind.

CHAPTER 17
Worship

W E LIVE IN a world where individuals constantly jockey for our attention. Everywhere we go, merchants want our business, people want our attention, social media outlets, streaming services, and networks want our eyes on them.

Why?

They want an investment from us, whether it be our money, time, energy, or all three. This fact alone doesn't make what they do good or bad; it's solely our choice where we invest our money, time, and energy. There are plenty of good things and plenty of bad things into which we can invest our time, energy, and resources.

For years, I believed a lie. I convinced myself that by investing my money, time, and energy into drugs and alcohol, I would get a valuable return on my investment. However, my real return was an increase in the customs and culture of the kingdom of darkness, which is nothing but chaos, misery, and a disconnect from the contentment and happiness only God can provide.

Here's the Good News, as described in Colossians 1:13, "*For he has rescued us from the kingdom of darkness and transferred us into the Kingdom of his dear Son.*" (NLT) Sadly, many people don't realize that what we pursue defines what we worship, and what we worship will have dominion over us.

As discussed in the last chapter, for years, I worshiped the lifestyle portrayed and promoted through rap music. I invested in this lifestyle and culture, and the return on my investment played out in tragic and disastrous ways.

I don't know what anyone else thinks when they hear the word *worship*, but it's safe to say that in our day and age, the word *worship* has lost much of its real meaning. Webster's Dictionary defines *Worship as: to honor or show reverence for a divine being or supernatural power; to regard with great or extravagant respect, honor, or devotion.*

The most common Old Testament word for worship is *shachah: to bow down.* The New Testament word adds a bit more insight. *Worship* in the Greek, *proskuneó: to do reverence to, to kiss the ground when prostrating before a superior; to worship, ready "to fall down/prostrate oneself to adore on one's knees."*

In many cultures across the world, and increasingly in American culture, we "worship" celebrities, politicians, athletes, video games, our work, and many other types of people and practices. We don't necessarily bow down and kiss these people's feet, but we often elevate them to a place where we *"regard [them] with great or extravagant respect, honor, or devotion."*

We have all, myself included, been inspired by people who fit these categories at times. However, following these people by investing large portions of our lives into what they say or do or following their lifestyle and habits is not likely to bring the best eternal return. Some of these people who inspire may even be following Jesus. Still, the Apostle Paul put it this way in regard to following and being inspired by mere people, *"Imitate me, just as I imitate Christ,"* 1 Corinthians 11:1 from the Amplified Bible. Paul is saying, if you're following me, make sure you're following the Jesus you see in me.

At this point in my new life, I was beginning to understand and experience true worship. I had begun to go to a non-denominational church and was starting to enjoy the uplifting, inspiring music at church. It was a wonderful change from my past form of worship.

I recall the first time Darin and Eileen asked me if I wanted to go to church. Everything in me said, "Nooooo!" But they began to tell me that I could wear shorts and sandals if I wanted and that it was very laid back. That sounded different from my experience with "church." The first time I went with them, the forty-five-minute car ride to Orange County was nerve-racking because of my memories of church. But there I was on my way to church one Sunday morning. To be honest, and to my surprise, I sort of enjoyed it.

Also, because I didn't have a grid for what "worshiping" was when the congregation began to sing, I thought we were just singing songs together for fun, but with no real purpose. Gradually, I looked forward to the "singing" part of the service at that Calvary Chapel in Orange County. Even then, I didn't fully grasp what was happening to me. I just knew that my life was slowly getting better.

Then, one night after a friend from work showed me some good worship music on YouTube, and after some months of enjoying the "singing" part of Sunday Service, I thought I'd give this "worship" music thing a try. So, one night alone at home, I pulled up that music on YouTube and sat in my bedroom.

With my attention and time focused on God, I intentionally "bowed down." In years past, I unknowingly did something similar, but with the distinct difference that the music I played then invited dark thinking and a dark presence. Subconsciously, I suppose I already had some understanding that music carried a spiritual reality and a presence, good or bad, with it.

I recalled an overwhelming presence filling my room. I recognized it in my mind and felt it in my body. Because I was intimately familiar with the presence of the enemy—being nervously revved up, feeling a heightened and tangible fear and paranoia all through my mind and body—I could easily distinguish the life-giving presence that filled my mind and rested on my body. It felt like perfect peace. The more I would worship, the more still I became, to the point I could barely move from my seat. All I wanted to do was smile, rest, and bask in God's presence.

It was like an invisible blanket settled in the room, and I was free from fear while under this covering. It was weighty, it was real, and it was comfortable. If you would have asked me to explain what was happening from a theological standpoint, I would not have been able to do so. I probably would have said, "I'm not entirely sure what's happening, but it has to be God because it's wonderful and peaceful." And just like that, I was hooked. I already had an addictive personality, so I was ready to embrace anything that made me feel truly good. This was a life-giving addiction, not a life-taking addiction. This was a golden investment, and the return on this investment was the reality of God's Kingdom slowly but surely expanding in my life. Romans 14:17 explains, *"For the kingdom of God is not eating and drinking, but righteousness and peace and joy in the Holy Spirit.* (NKJV) The presence filling my room was that of the dominion of the King of Kings. Right living, peace, and joy are the return on investment in His Kingdom.

As I worshiped the One that loves us and gave His life for us, slowly but surely, my mind started being renewed, and as I grew closer to Him. He made me more aware of how much He loves each of His children. Also, little did I know then that worshiping God is like wielding a weapon at the darkness that tries to consume us. I was about to experience this in a dramatic way.

Having lived through the spiritual, emotional, and physical torment of addiction, it wasn't hard for me to mentally grab hold of the fact that there is a battle between light and dark, angels and demons, God and the devil. I had long experienced this reality. Even today, having talked with thousands of people caught in the fight or coming out of the spiritual battle of addiction, most have little problem understanding that while spiritual forces of darkness may not be visible, they are as real as the air we breathe. I was about to get a crash course in this reality.

Darin, Eileen, and I left one Sunday morning and headed to a 10:30 a.m. church service. We settled in on the third row to the left side of the stage, and I recall being joyfully engaged from the start.

The lights dimmed, and the band became energized as the congregation engaged. But I noticed quickly that something was different about this Sunday morning. As I joined the singing and connected my heart to the presence of God, it was as if a swell of stormy seas began rising within me. One song passed, and the internal tension increased. As the worship team transitioned to another song, I had to sit down, and I slumped into my seat. Immediately, my mind began racing like a movie on fast forward as dark thoughts careened through my mind, "What in the world is this?" I interjected into the chaos as my thoughts screamed, telling me I should leave the sanctuary and sit in the hallway. I refused and tried to stay engaged and focused on God. I didn't know what was going on, but it felt like my inner world was a ship at sea trying to withstand fifty-foot waves brought on by hurricane-force winds. My upper body and head began rocking back and forth like I was dancing in a mosh pit. I could feel an unseen force clawing on me and trying to get me to leave this environment.

I refused even though I felt like I had little to no control. As my upper body and head rocked, I began squeezing my head. Darin leaned over and said, "You ok man?" I couldn't respond. I tried my hardest to keep worshiping God during a real but unseen battle. I can only imagine what I looked like to the churchgoers around me. Here I was, pursuing God and desiring more and more of Him in my life, and all of a sudden, I looked and began behaving like I belonged in the psych ward. Add to this wild scene the fact that this particular church doesn't even believe in this kind of supernatural activity. Yet here I was, being delivered from demons by the Holy Spirit on the third row of their church.

The tension continued to press on me, and my thoughts continued to race as darkness seemed to be overtaking me. It wasn't actually so. I understand now that what was happening was that the might of God was overtaking darkness. The enemy wasn't winning, but he sure was kicking and screaming on his way out, like a toddler does when he doesn't get his or her way at playtime.

Then, in a moment, just as the intensity of the experience was climaxing, it stopped. It was as if all the stormy seas were made still in a moment. I felt the dark, chaotic presence leave. While it was greatly relieving, it was also a little bizarre. Faster than the whole ordeal started, it was over, and I sat there, not knowing what to think or do.

My first thoughts were, "What was that, and what are those around me thinking of me right now?" As I refused to give in to this evil spirit, the Holy Spirit Himself began evicting the demonic thoughts and spirit that came upon me. I didn't understand what had happened until months later, after processing the whole situation and talking with someone who knew more about deliverance.

I sat through the service feeling bewildered. Even after the madness was gone, I wanted to sit in the lobby and recuperate. Instead, I just sat through the service like a sailor who almost drowned but was rescued at the last moment.

Time and time again, we see Jesus in the Gospels casting demons out of people. *"The Spirit of the Lord is upon Me, Because He anointed Me to bring good news to the poor. He has sent Me to proclaim release to captives, And recovery of sight to the blind, To set free those who are oppressed."* (Isaiah 61:1)

It seems foolish to think that in our day, demons have ceased to exist. Yet, the same battle is still raging in the unseen realm, and the same Jesus is still winning the battle against darkness.

One of the most well-known stories of deliverance from demons occurred when Jesus set a man free from *"legions"* of demons. As Jesus stepped off the boat, a man possessed with many demons ran to Him and *"worshiped Him."* Jesus cast the demons out of this man.

As I sat in that church, I didn't have a "Legion" of demons in me (a legion in Roman military parlance describes a unit of more than six thousand men). Yet, for years, I had been hiding in the shadows and partaking in deeds of darkness, and by doing so, I welcomed dark spirits into my internal world. I was unaware of what I was doing. Nevertheless, by living that lifestyle, I opened the door and gave access to the demonic realm to enter my house—to dominate my spirit.

When the man possessed with demons saw Jesus and *"ran to him and threw himself down before him,"* the man didn't have the power to free himself. But as he worshiped The One that came to *"proclaim release to captives [and]...set free those who are oppressed,"* the Master freed him from captivity.

My experience was not as climactic, but the same Jesus that set that man free set me free that day as I worshiped at His feet. Never forget Jesus is on a mission. His mission hasn't changed, and He continues to accomplish His mission through His Spirit and His believers. His mission is to set captives free from spiritual bondage and to love them into an abundant life, a life of peace, freedom, and purpose, *"Now the*

Lord is the Spirit, and where the Spirit of the Lord is, there is freedom." (2 Cor. 3:17, NASB)

A few nasty addictions remained a year into my recovery from drugs and alcohol. But shortly after this powerful deliverance, a fourteen-year pornography addiction departed from my life. In that same window of time, my addiction to cigarettes was won as well.

And if I thought I was free before, what was coming next was even better. A whole new world was about to open up to me.

CHAPTER 18

More On Identity

RR

W E LIVE IN a culture where our worth and significance are primarily based on our performance. What's the first question we get asked when we meet someone for the first time? It's almost always, "What do you do?"

We reply with our best-polished answer and mindlessly ask, "And what do you do?" It's not all shallow and bad. I get it. It's a widely accepted and simple way for us to get to know each other. But how confused would someone be if you asked them, "Who are you beyond your name and title?"

I think most people would probably be caught off guard by a question like that. It's been my experience that most people find their identity in their titles and accomplishments, their earnings, and the image they've created of themselves. This cultural norm often continues its shallowness. When we see an old friend or acquaintance and ask, "How have you been?" The most common reply I hear is, "I've just been so busy," followed by rattling off everything they've been doing. I'll admit that I've done this.

It should go without saying, but I'll say it. Our accomplishments are part of who we are. I love setting goals and seeing them through.

God even rewards us based upon our actions, or you could say accomplishments. (See Matthew 6:25-34) But how many of us lose focus and exhaust ourselves by basing our worth and identity solely on what we've accomplished rather than what God has accomplished in us and through us?

Again, some of these measuring sticks are warranted. If a business sees potential in a possible employee and hires them, they can't keep that employee forever if the person isn't performing sufficiently at the job they were hired to do. To stay in business, you must make a profit, and employees who don't contribute to your success can become a liability--that's the function of a business.

But is that same approach appropriate when spending time with friends and family, or is it appropriate in how we portray ourselves to the world? The world seems to think so, but there is Good News. God does not operate this way.

Try thinking about this for a moment. Let's say that Jesus hadn't come yet, and we knew the prophecies about Him and were awaiting His arrival. Upon arriving, who do you think He would pick to carry His glory? I think it's safe to say many people would expect Him to gravitate to the most influential people because they could reach the most people right from the start due to their wide sphere of influence. We would probably think He would pick the most accomplished and successful people because they've proven they can succeed. We wouldn't be surprised if He picked the most polished people because we're talking about people who will be carrying the *name above all names*. Did He do that when he first came to earth? No, we know unequivocally He did not choose those types of people for His original starting lineup. Instead, He picked a ragtag bunch of rowdy "sinners," and most had accomplished very little in worldly success.

What is that about? Well, God is a masterful artist. Have you ever seen the sunsets with which He fills the horizons? Have you ever experienced the beauty of the natural world, exquisite even down to the smallest detail? Have you considered the intricacies and wonders of the human body? Why would He pick what the world would deem broken and dull tools to paint His tapestry of love and glory on earth?

Out of His abounding love for us, He has answered this question in the apostle Paul's letter to the Corinthians,

"But God chose those whom the world considers foolish to shame those who think they are wise, and God chose the puny and powerless to shame the high and mighty. He chose the lowly, the laughable in the world's eyes—nobodies—so that he would shame the somebodies. For he chose what is regarded as insignificant in order to supersede what is regarded as prominent, so that there would be no place for prideful boasting in God's presence. For it is not from man that we draw our life but from God as we are being joined to Jesus, the Anointed One." (1 Corinthians 1:27-31, TPT) How much more glory God gets, and rightfully so, when He displays His wisdom, power, and love through people that the world deems lost and broken fools.

God didn't come to me and say, "Hi Erik. Nice to meet you. What do you do for a living?" It sounds silly to even think He would. He came to me and said, "Follow me." He certainly wasn't impressed with my worldly accomplishments.

He sees our humility and willingness to obey Him. He sees who we can become as we let Him live in our hearts. He sees who He created us to be in light of His transformative grace and unending love. He sees who we will become once we are washed clean through His finished work on the cross.

During this season of my life, God again changed the topics of the conversations He and I were having. The aim of these new conversations was for me to truly begin to understand who I am in Him. The first topic of these discussions was about leaving A.A. "Wait, what?" At first, I was certain that this recurring thought was not God. "There's no way. I'm an alcoholic. I'll go straight back to the insanity of addiction if I leave AA." But God didn't relent.

As I slowly started to entertain the idea that maybe it was God, He elaborated ideas to me in a discourse on freedom, "If you continue to subscribe to AA's way of thinking, there will always be a ceiling on your growth in Me." I didn't understand initially, but I leaned into this directive.

Shortly after that, an experience with Him captured my consciousness. I was sitting on the beach in Oceanside, CA, pondering a Bible passage I'd read that morning. *"Every single moment you are thinking of me! How precious and wonderful to consider that you cherish me constantly in your every thought! O God, your desires toward me are more than the grains of sand on every shore! When I awake each morning, you're still with me."* (Psalm 139: 17–18, TPT)

Am I, are you, really that precious to God? As I sat with my shoes off and my feet nestled in the sand, I gazed more closely at the soft California sand. Reaching down, I pinched a dime-sized amount of those minute powdered pebbles between my thumb and index finger and sprinkled it into my palm, letting it trickle through my fingers like sand going through an hourglass.

As I did so, I contemplated how many individual grains of sand were in just the minuscule pile I'd cradled. I couldn't even begin to guess that number, though it was probably far more than I would have thought. Still locked in the moment, I gazed down the sandy shoreline in awe and wondered, "How many billions or trillions of sand particles are on the beaches of Southern California alone?" My thoughts turned to God, and I asked, "How is it even possible to have that many thoughts, let alone have that many good thoughts about me?"

I looked again at my hand, recalling the sand I'd held there. My mind shifted to the nails driven through the hands and feet of Christ. God was granting me a tiny glimpse into how He thought and felt about me and all of us. We are so valuable to Him that He allowed His Son to be sacrificed on our behalf. *"For the joy set before him [Christ] endured the cross,"* the writer of Hebrews reminds us. What's the "joy set before Him?" You and I were the joy set before Him. Redeeming humanity back to our rightful place of forgiven and unbroken union with the Father was the joy that fueled Christ through the most horrific and brutal suffering in human history.

He saw my value long before I accomplished anything. He saw goodness in me before I could even entertain the idea that there was goodness inside me. He saw a future friend when He gazed into my lost and broken heart. When demons dwelled in me, He saw a house fit for a King. He knew all my issues and still saw the eternal significance and divine potential within me. He knew all of it, and He still invited me to join Him on the journey of growing into who He knew I could become. He asked me to follow Him into the unknown and trust that He is the *Author and finisher of my faith*.

He sees us all this way. That's what His work on the cross accomplished, and when we see our intrinsic worth through the lens of what Jesus did on our behalf, we begin to understand how priceless we are. We begin to set out to fulfill our God-given calling. As we do so, He empowers us to work *from* a place of victory and significance, not *for* a victory and a place of significance.

Do you know what the reality of knowing how precious we are to God does to someone who has lived their life in an invisible prison of spiritual torment? The phrase "life-changing" doesn't quite do it justice. God didn't just change my life. The old me died, and He gave me a brand-new life in Him and through Him. As explained in Romans 6:11, "*So you also must consider yourselves dead to sin and alive to God in Christ Jesus.* (ESV)

How many good thoughts about you and I were racing through Jesus' mind as the nails were driven through His hands and feet? I sat on that Southern California beach, trying to wrap my head around what seemed like an atomic bomb exploding in my mind.

Our conversation continued as God indicated, "Start taking ownership of my character traits. You were created in my image *and likeness*. Your potential is unlimited." These thoughts had never entered my mind, but the more I allowed God to establish His reality, the more I saw His characteristics in my life.

"I'm an alcoholic" is the declaration every person makes when they enter the AA fellowship. "Let's chat about this, son," I heard in my mind. "How is it that you can be an alcoholic when the old you is dead, and I have resurrected you as a brand-new creation? Understand that Christ didn't go through what He went through on the cross so that you would hold onto a false identity based on inherent sinfulness." Again, how do you respond to God after He says that? Other than, "Ah, you're right—as always."

These types of conversations were constant for a season. God zeroed in on breaking me free from the mindsets that served me well for a season but would cap my growth in Him as my journey continued.

God used the AA fellowship as a powerful and critical stepping stone in my life, but He now wanted me to move from the stepping stone to The Cornerstone, Christ Jesus. A new chapter was beginning, and just as God did when I started this journey, He brought amazing people into my life for this new chapter. This time, He brought people who knew the Holy Spirit into my life. These were people my age, and they were fun and crazy in all the right ways.

CHAPTER 19
Miracles

W HAT IS A miracle? Before I dive into that, let's start here.
On Sept. 19, 1866, a man named Alfred Nobel submitted
a patent application for "Dynamite or Nobel's Safety
Powder." The name Nobel might ring a bell, the Nobel Peace Prize.
Yes, the Nobel Peace Prize was named after the inventor of dynamite.

Nobel, the holder of 355 patents over the course of his life, was
also a builder in his hometown of Stockholm, Sweden. He envisioned
dynamite being used to clear rocks, tunnels, railways, and so on. But its
biggest usage early on was for warfare, first used in 1870 in the Franco-
German war. It became widespread for cannon use shortly after that.

Although it was used extensively for warfare, dynamite was used
more for mining and its initial intention of clearing away areas for
roads, tunnels, railways, and the like. Still, to this day, dynamite is used
in mining, big construction projects, and demolition.

The Swedish inventor Nobel also invented the word *dynamite,*
originally *dynamit.* Derived from the Greek word *dunamis,* we will dive
more into this momentarily. *Dunamis* is also where our English word
for *dynasty* comes from, meaning a family or group that wields power
over several generations.

Why is all this important?

The word miracles in Greek is *dunamis - miraculous power, might, strength.* We could say that miracles are the dynamite power of God that reveals the heavenly realm in the earthly realm.

Many of us can get behind the idea of someone's life being transformed as a miracle, as we should. God's dynamite power certainly exploded in my life and blew hell out of the premises. Seeing someone's life go from chaos to complete transformation in Christ is miraculous. That is the power of God on display. What bigger miracle is there than seeing salvation, complete wholeness of life, come into a lost and broken soul?

At that time, I began to think, "If God is all-powerful, and if He can change my dark heart, what more can He do?" I'd read the stories of Jesus performing miracles, and my fascination with this King of Kings only increased.

How does Webster define the word *miracle*? A miracle is "*an unusual or wonderful event that is believed to be caused by the power of God.*"

The word used for a miracle in the Bible is used in many ways. Here is one verse where the word is used. Mark 6:2 - *And when the Sabbath came, He began to teach in the synagogue; and the many listeners were astonished, saying, "Where did this man learn these things, and what is this wisdom that has been given to Him, and such miracles as these performed by His hands?* (NASB)

Miracles have a way of challenging the faithless mind. My experience has been that most human beings tend to criticize and shy away from what they don't understand and, many times, what they can't control. God's miraculous power cannot be controlled and can be hard for someone whose mind hasn't been renewed to understand. Even the renewed mind will need to embrace some mystery when it comes to the dynamite power of God breaking into our finite world.

But I was just crazy enough, and still am, to believe God is exactly who He says He is. Jesus Himself told us to pray this way: Matthew 6:10 *Your kingdom come. Your will be done On earth as it is in heaven.* Just three verses later, Jesus ends that prayer with, "*For Yours is the kingdom and the power and the glory forever. Amen.*" (NKJV) The word for *power* is, you guessed it, *dunamis*. The King Himself directed us to pray for the dynamite power of God to be revealed here on earth.

I would discover these passages during that window of time and read these verses and say to myself, "I believe you, God. I may not be seeing your Kingdom fully manifesting in my world yet, but I believe you. Bring it about in my world." If Jesus Himself told us to pray for God's *Dunamis* power to be displayed through the believer's life, what right do I have not to pursue and believe God? The Bible says, "*miraculous signs will accompany those who believe,*" in Mark 16:17.

What did all this mean for me, and was I to think that a Holy and Perfect God would pick me to reveal His power and glory? Who am I to say I have a right to pick who God can and can't use? Furthermore, what right do I have to say that God doesn't use His kids to reveal His dynamite power? He's the One who said, "*Jesus Christ is the same yesterday and today, and forever.*" (Heb. 13:8 NASB)

This heavenly whirlwind was so strong in my life that I didn't stop to try and think myself out of any of this. I just kept moving in the direction that His wind was taking me. The enemy had used me to accomplish his tasks for years. I wanted to see the dynamite power of heaven through my life. Anyone who knew me from my past already thought I was crazy. What did I possibly have to lose? Nothing, I had nothing to lose, and I had God's entire Kingdom to gain. I just kept pursuing Jesus, the real Jesus portrayed throughout the four gospels.

At this point in my short journey, God had already placed me around true believers who were helping me grow in a life of the Spirit. This was roughly two years into this metamorphosis. In this window, I began to recognize how many people were healed in the three-and-a-half-year period of Jesus' public ministry. It's constant throughout all four gospels. I started seeing how He cast out demons everywhere He went and how He would hear God in detail and relay His words to the world around Him. Seeing this was like a stick of dynamite going off inside of me.

I then learned that Jesus said, "*Heal the sick, raise the dead, cleanse those with leprosy, cast out demons. Freely you received, freely give.*" Matt. 10:8 (NASB) This made sense to my windy mind. God had brought me through too much. I had experienced too much of His power and grace to stop short of the real adventure with Jesus, which brings His world into this one.

So, what did I do? I started praying for people everywhere I went. I started believing that the same Jesus I read about in the Bible lived inside me and wanted to use my life to accomplish the same works He accomplished in the Gospels. *1 John 2:6 Whoever claims to live in him must live as Jesus did. (NIV)*

God had brought me to the point where it sounded crazy to me not to start pursuing this life of dunamis power. Jesus said, *"As you go,"* so I started wherever I was. Before I knew Jesus, I brought hell to earth as I went about my daily life. It was now time to bring heaven to earth.

So, it began. The first person I laid hands on and prayed for was my old sponsor. He had been having horrible headaches and trouble sleeping. I just did what I was taught and prayed like Jesus. I simply laid my hands on him, commanded the headaches to go in Jesus' name, and prayed for perfect sleep.

I'd seen people pray for others for healing, and I had participated in group prayers for people who needed healing. But this was the first time I was doing it on my own. I felt weird, to be honest, but my desire to see God at work trumped any fear that was trying to stop me. There was no big immediate sign from heaven, just faith that my simple act of obedience would release heaven's dynamite.

Sometime later, I timidly asked him about his headaches and sleep. He told me he hadn't had a headache since I prayed for him and was also sleeping great.

I was so excited I started praying for more people. Not everyone was healed, but I was seeing people healed. And the more I obeyed God's mandate of *healing the sick,* the more people I saw healed. It's all Him. He's just looking for willing vessels. It got to the point where everyone who needed to be healed at my work was healed, as I would just pray for them at work. I began to see people give their lives to Jesus as a result of them being healed.

It was like a heavenly tornado touched down in my life, but this Wind brought healing, this Wind brought restoration, this Wind brought peace, and joy, and this Wind came to fix problems, not create them.

Like I said at the beginning of the chapter, dynamite was used for warfare and, more so, to clear away obstructions so building and expansion could occur. It was also used extensively, and still is, for mining precious metals like gold, silver, copper, and so on.

Heaven's dynamite is the same. God's power comes to remove the blockages that the enemy has brought into children's lives. God's miraculous power mines the precious treasures out of us so that our true identity can rise to the surface, and this Dunamis reality comes to empower us to confront the forces of hell with unstoppable weapons—God's power and love. The enemy's work, which resembles death, loss, or destruction, is overturned and restored as God's Dunamis power brings healing, restoration, redemption, and wholeness to our lives.

I was possessed with the message of God's grace, power, and love. It seemed like a normal response to what God had brought me through. I had been set free from the portable and invisible prison of hell on earth. All the offenses that rightfully kept me in that dark cell were canceled, and all their effects were null and void.

Not only that, that old person was now dead, and a new person was alive in me, filled with the Spirit of an all-powerful and loving God. Do you know what that does to someone? I'll tell you; it makes them crazy in all the right ways. I began to walk down the streets and see people living in that prison that I was so familiar with for all those years, and I couldn't help myself. I had to pray for their freedom and tell them about the King of Kings.

One night, after leaving a meeting where my friends and I were worshiping Jesus and praying, I became hungry for a California Burrito. If you haven't had a Cali burrito from a hole-in-the-wall Mexican food joint in southern California, you are missing a piece of heaven on earth.

On this night, I was on a mission and found the nearest burrito spot. I entered, and there were very few people in this small restaurant. I wasn't trying to be super spiritual. I wasn't thinking of praying for the cashier, either. I was on a mission to experience some late-night heaven on earth through a California Burrito.

As I ordered and sat down to enjoy the food, God began speaking to me. Holy Spirit told me that He wanted me to tell the young man working that night that He was proud of him for the decisions he was making to better his life. So first, I finished my burrito, of course, and then I stopped to speak with this young man on my way out.

I didn't add any weirdness to the situation, and I didn't use church language. I simply went up to him and said, "Hey, man. This might sound strange, but I just love God, and He loves people, and I felt like He wanted me to tell you something." He looked at me, puzzled but intrigued. He replied, "Okay, sure. What's up?"

I said, "I feel like God just wants you to know that He is proud of you. I feel like you made some good decisions recently, and God wants you to know that He sees you and has good things in store for you." The young man immediately responded, "No way! I don't believe this, no way!" I laughed and asked him to explain what was going on. He said, "Today, I threw my weed away and prayed that God would help me change my life. This is crazy!"

He then told me he felt "the chills" all over his body. What was happening? God's miraculous power, dunamis, had come to earth, and God was answering a prayer and revealing Himself to one of His children.

I asked him what he thought about all of it. He was excited and happy, to say the least. I told him, "This God that you were talking with earlier today, and this feeling that you're feeling all over your body right now, what if this could live inside of you every day?" He said, "What?" I continued and told him about my testimony and what God had done in my life.

I went on, "Yeah, man. What if this God you're experiencing right now lived inside of you? Would you want that?" He rapidly replied, "Yes, yes, I would." I told him to give me his hand, and I had him pray a simple prayer of faith for Jesus to forgive him and come and live inside His heart. I then had him ask the Holy Spirit to fill him. As he asked for the Holy Spirit to fill him, he said, "I feel warm. My whole body is feeling warm and tingly from the inside out."

I finished praying with him and explained that the warmth he was experiencing was God's Spirit coming to dwell inside Him. He looked different after this experience. This young man was visibly joyful and more energetic. I told him about the church I knew of right around the corner. I told him to go to church, tell the pastor what had happened, and get connected there.

These types of things began happening just about daily. I wasn't going out to "evangelize," and I never knew what would happen. I just went about my days knowing Jesus was with me, proclaiming His Kingdom was at hand and giving Him a chance to be who He says He is to the world around me.

I went from being a drug addict and alcoholic to God using me to set drug addicts and alcoholics free. I went from needing healing to being someone God used to heal people. I went from wandering in the darkness to being set free and carrying His Light back into the darkness.

What the enemy used for bad in my life, God flipped the script and brought good out of it like only He can.

This hasn't stopped. I continued as we would go into nightclubs, and people were healed and saved, in businesses, schools, churches, and as we went in public. I took teams into the redlight district of Tijuana, Mexico, for two years. And the entire time, Jesus did and has done what only He can do. He does miracles. He lights the fuses in us so His heavenly dynamite can explode through us into the world around us.

CHAPTER 20
Led By the Spirit

RR

W HAT WAS NEXT?
It was hard to process the details of God's transformative grace in real time as it flooded my life. He was saying so much and doing so much in my life, and I was captivated in the moments when it occurred. I was just trying to keep pace with processing new experiences and encounters with God. At times, it felt like I was being whipped around like a leaf in the wind, but at least now I was being whipped and blown in the right direction.

My family and I lived in rural Ohio for two and a half years. Ohio has great people but pretty atrocious weather from the point of view of someone who lived most of their life in the sunny state of California. Ohio rains around 133 days a year and averages one sunny day in three. The average year-round temperature is 53 degrees. Since my wife and I grew up living close to and spending time at the beach, we were very happy that God moved us to southwest Florida in June 2020.

One day, however, while living in rural Carroll County, Ohio, we enjoyed pizza in our backyard with our boys when the city sirens went off. Small towns in Ohio still have very loud sirens that warn people when tornados and storms are coming. I had never experienced a tornado, although the sirens had gone off before, followed by very anticlimactic weather.

So, on this day, I didn't think much of the siren wails and even joked to our two boys, "Oh no, a huge tornado is coming!" They laughed, aware of sirens going off before, followed by no tornado.

This time was different. The sirens continued, and we got an update on our phones stating a tornado watch was in the area. This wasn't the first time that had happened either, but then the wind began blowing a little harder.

We continued to sit and eat pizza. I even joked with my boys about the sissy tornado coming through our little town of three thousand people. Almost immediately, stiff winds caught the lids on the pizza boxes and nearly blew them off the table. Surprised, my wife and I looked at each other and quickly agreed that going inside was probably a good idea.

Before we even finished getting the boys and pizza inside the house, monstrous but unseen forces of wind were blowing so hard it affected our balance as we got inside. Within minutes, we were in a tornado. I was still making jokes about it—perhaps I was in denial, and I couldn't comprehend what was happening, having never been in a tornado—yet all the while, shingles from our roof were being ripped away and dispersed across our nearly acre size lot. This type of storm was new to me, and it came fast. One moment, we were enjoying pleasant weather by Ohio's standards. Next, a siren warned us of impending tornado-force winds, and within moments it was upon us.

Curious but foolish, I opened the front door at one point in the peak of the storm, still unable to fully process what was happening. Before I got it part way open, the wind forced me back, and I lost my handle on the door. It blew wide open. Leaves and rain swirled forward, rushing into our house. Using the full force of my weight to fight against the wind, I finally managed to wrestle it closed. We gathered and hunkered down in a safe place.

The tornado didn't last long, maybe four to five minutes, and it was over as quickly as it seemed to descend upon us.

Luckily, we were among those that didn't experience major damage to our house or yard. Broken-off branches, shingles, and a few outside things were flung about our yard. However, a mile or so away, a woman's trailer told a different, tragic story. On a drive the next day, we observed that the force of the winds had literally picked up her trailer and flipped it on its side. Thank goodness she was not home when it happened.

In the Bible, we often see the word "Spirit" or the phrase "Spirit of God." What does that mean? What does the invisible activity of an all-powerful God look like in our little lives? A little deeper exploration can aid our understanding. In the Old Testament (Hebrew), we see the word Spirit, *Ruach*: breath, wind, spirit. In the New Testament (Greek), we see the word Spirit, *Pneuma*: wind, breath, spirit. Note the same definitions, yet through different languages from different cultures and different time periods.

How many times in my life, before I knew Jesus, did I feel, spiritually speaking, like a wind was blowing me in directions I shouldn't or did not want to go? Countless nights during my years of insanity included wind blowing through my mind, carrying thoughts of partying. What I believed was fun was a wind that led to drug and alcohol consumption for well over a decade. This dark, with sometimes hurricane-force gales, drove me deeper and deeper into darkness.

For far too many years, I found no shelter from the winds of darkness that blew so ferociously in my life. It wasn't until I found refuge in Jesus that they no longer produced the same effects. When we submit to the sweet, gentle whispering, and occasionally even attention-grabbing current of God's Spirit, it doesn't just move us in the right direction. It also shields us from the taunting Satanic breezes that can quickly turn into hurricane-force winds in our lives.

Our house in that storm in Ohio was our refuge from the tornado that descended on our community, just as Christ can be our refuge against the spiritual and emotional storms we will each confront. The Savior became a protective, life-saving shelter against the winds of darkness. The Old Testament prophet Isaiah understood this: "*You [Jesus] have been a fortress-protector for the poor, a mighty stronghold for the needy in their distress, a shelter from the sudden storm, and a shade from the shimmering heat of the day. For the fury of tyrants was like a winter windstorm battering against the wall.*" (Isaiah 25:5, Passion Translation)

Jesus described this new life of living in His breath, His wind, and His Spirit in an exchange with a curious religious man named Nicodemus, who was among an elite body of Jewish religious leaders.

When Nicodemus said to Jesus, *"How can a person be born when he is old? He cannot enter his mother's womb a second time and be born, can he?" Jesus answered, "Truly, truly, I say to you, unless someone is born of water **and the Spirit**, he cannot enter the kingdom of God. That which has been born of the flesh is flesh, and that which has been born of the Spirit is spirit. Do not be amazed that I said to you, 'You must be born again.' The wind blows where it wishes, and you hear the sound of it, but you do not know where it is coming from and where it is going; so is everyone who has been born of the Spirit."* (John 3:4-8, NASB)

Although a religious leader, Nicodemus was not able to understand the message Jesus shared with him as Christ attempted to use a metaphor to explain that the Spirit of God is all around us to guide us and direct us if we will but listen and obey — if we will be "born again," or "born from above." Their conversation continued. Nicodemus responded to Jesus, *"How can these things be? Jesus answered and said to him, "You are the teacher of Israel, and yet you do not understand these things? Truly, truly, I say to you, we speak of what we know and testify of what we have seen, and you people do not accept our testimony. If I told you earthly things and you do not believe, how will you believe if I tell you heavenly things?* (John 3:9-12, NASB)

Nicodemus was an elite religious leader and teacher of "Godly things" in Judaism. Yet he and other leaders were essentially "the blind leading the blind" because they did not comprehend the foundational reality and importance of living a life led by the Holy Spirit. A life of being *"born from above"* is a life of being born into the Spirit, Wind, and Breath of God. We can only understand life in His Spirit by knowing Him and His Word, and experiencing His reality in us and through us. At this time, it seemed Nicodemus could not comprehend that Jesus Christ was the Son of God, called to bring life and light to the world, because Nicodemus had not yet been born into this life and Spirit.

This new Wind began sheltering me and blowing me deeper into God and an abundant life as I followed Him. But what does life being led by the Spirit look like? It's simple: It looks like the life Jesus lived.

No, not perfection and walking on water (although I'd love to do that), but a life led by the Spirit should include right living in the eyes of God. It should include joy, being a peacemaker, extending grace to others, loving the unlovable, and returning kindness in the face of anger. It should include miracles, healing, and the many other characteristics Jesus personified during his life. *This is the normal life of a follower of Jesus.*

One of the things that helped me stay on this path early in my journey was helping others. Friends and mentors who had walked the path of recovery before me encouraged me to serve others, knowing it was vital to remain on the path to freedom. I followed their advice, especially because assisting others is clearly enjoined by God in the Bible and was the very essence of Christ's life.

At this time, I was working at a fish and chips joint in North San Diego County. I worked the night shift most of the time, and we always had leftover food at the end of the night. I was looking to serve others, and it was a no-brainer for me to gather up any leftover fried fish, fries, and soup (almost always clam chowder) and take it down to the homeless kids who lived by the pier in Oceanside.

Oceanside had a huge transient population when I lived there, largely because of its location and temperate year-round weather. I'd finish my work shifts with food in hand and head down to the darkness under the pier to deliver leftovers and pray for my friends there. I never looked at it as if it were some kind of religious duty or something that deserved a reward. This whole action sprang from knowing Jesus and doing my best to do what He said, "*Do to others what you would have them do to you.*" (Matt. 7:12). "Well, I'd want someone to do that for me if I was homeless," was my simple thought in response to Jesus' directive.

In doing this, I got to know the people that lived on the streets. I knew their names and some of their stories. Most nights, they would be waiting for me and the free food. They called me "The clam chowder guy." I'd sit with them while they'd eat and tell them what God had done in my life. I'd pray for them and encourage them, promising that their lives could get better. I didn't have any training on handing out food to homeless people or talking with people living on the streets.

What I did have was an understanding of what many of their lives were like because I'd "been there and done that." More importantly, I had a heart transformed by God and a heavenly wind blowing me to do what I was doing. I started with what I had. I had God, and I had time, and He multiplied what I had and what I could do.

God combined a little bit of my free time with my desire to feed the hungry and open hearts with food and words. As I did so, God granted me more wisdom on how to talk with hurting people. He gave me more resources to help get the job done. My simple act of willingness sparked a whirlwind of God's power and love in my little life and the lives of others. I soon found myself going to the pier area a few times a week in my spare time to hang out with these beautiful people. I found purpose in my life the more I focused on helping others succeed. I better understood God's love for me as I intentionally loved others with Him.

I drove my new friends to places they needed to be and prayed for their lives to be transformed. Some of them gave their lives to Jesus, got healed, and got off the streets. I knew what Jesus had done for me and that if He could change my life, He could change their lives. It became my passion to help them understand what Jesus could and would do for them as they turned to Him.

After a few months, heaven's wind picked up speed in my world. I found myself inviting others onto the streets to help those in need so they could experience the joy I felt.

Before I knew God, the enemy's wind had me roaming the streets up to no good. Now, the wind of God had me roaming the streets doing good. No surprise, but God had flipped the script on the enemy, *"And we know that God causes everything to work together for the good of those who love God and are called according to his purpose for them."* Romans 8:28 (NLT)

God's wind continued blowing doors open as I found myself being invited to speak in churches and home groups and share what God had done in my life and what He was doing through my life. I spoke about Jesus Christ and His grace. The places I avoided at all costs in the past were now where I testified of Him and His love for each of us. Only God could do such a thing.

It was as if a heavenly tornado descended on my life and blew my entire world in a dramatically different direction before I fully realized what was happening. And each time that joyous wind blew in my life, it left me longing for more. I hungered to see and know more. I wanted the real Jesus in my life and nothing less than that. It became the main focus of my life.

CHAPTER 21
You Are More Valuable Than You Realize

RR

R OUGHLY FOUR OR five hundred years ago in Japan, a beautiful process for repairing ceramics arose. This process is called "kintsugi." Kintsugi means "golden seams" or "golden repair." Stories vary on the exact origins of Kintsugi. Only a rough estimate as to when it started is known for sure. The process goes as such. When a bowl or any sort of ceramic piece is broken, it is not thrown away. Instead, it is repaired, but not in a way that the world has ever seen. When a piece is broken, they take it and piece it back together with a gold lacquer.

They believe that the value of the ceramic piece is not lost, nor do they want to lose its memories. So, instead of tossing it to the wayside, they repair the piece with a substance that adds value to the broken areas. If you look up Kintsugi pictures, you will see beautiful bowls that were broken and then put back together. You can see where it was broken because gold is the glue that brings the piece back to wholeness. This process elevates the broken areas into being more visible and valuable than the areas that were never broken.

All the memories and conversations that were had while the family spent time together over meals and all the delicious food eaten out of that bowl made that bowl have far more value than just a tool to eat. The Japanese can see this, and they would rather keep the bowl and its memories by gluing it back together with a substance that financially costs far more than the bowl itself, but to them, the sentiment that the bowl carries is worth more than the bowl.

God is no different. He doesn't see us as worthless and destroyed when we are broken. He sees an opportunity for His love and the finished work of Christ to bring us back together. He sees how His love and grace can add value to the broken areas and put us on display as a trophy of His grace.

I used to ask myself, "Why me?"

Love. He loves me, the same that He loves you. He sees what could and can be. He sees how my life can bring hope to those who believe they are broken beyond repair. He sees the treasure that He buried deep in my heart and longs to bring it out and give it away to the world around me. His desire for you is the same.

As you've read, I didn't have all my ducks in a row when He came to me. I still haven't achieved perfection. But Love Himself sees the value in His creation even if His creation can't see the value in itself. He saw my little life and said, "I love you, and I will love you, and the divine potential I placed in you will rise to the surface." He is looking at you and saying the same thing, "Let me love you."

He didn't love me into this transformation to get me to be His busy little religious servant. He just loved me, and loved me, and still loves me. And as I experienced His love, I have been compelled to tell and show the world the love He has for them. It's a never-ending love story.

This isn't my plan for my life. This is His plan for my life.

As I hear His voice, it changes me. As His wind blows in my life, it takes the parts of me that He never intended to be there. As His living waters run through me, it washes away the residue of my past dead life.

The part of my story I told in the last chapter was roughly ten years ago. Since then, the journey and the adventure have continued, and more books will tell those stories.

This journey we are on promises challenges, tough seasons, testing, and trials. But it also promises joy, peace, and prosperity in all aspects of life.

Your journey is far from over. The Author of Life has ways of bringing glorious plot twists into our reality. As God's winds of change begin to blow in your life, will you trust His Spirit is leading you into His abundant life? As He opens doors and makes space for you in rooms you don't feel you belong, will you trust that He has gone before you to make a way for you? As new healthy relationships enter your life, will you trust that God is working inside these people to help you?

Jesus longs to walk with you, talk with you, and guide you into an abundant life of freedom. I can see Jesus sitting on a bench at the beginning of a long trail that heads into the wild. As you approach the trail, He gazes up into the depths of your soul with warm and joyful eyes. He says with a soft and confident tone, "Ready to go on this adventure with Me?" "But Jesus," you anxiously reply. He interrupts your fearful discourse with, "We will have plenty of time to talk on this adventure. Trust me, and follow me into the life you were born for."

He sits with an overwhelming confidence in His ability to transform your life and allows you to choose. Time stands still, and you glance behind you as the past pulls on your soul. You then gaze into His eyes as tears begin to slowly roll down your cheeks. As The Prince of Peace stands to His feet and extends His hand to you, He says, "I love you. Let's go on an adventure."

About the Author

ERIK AND HIS beautiful wife, Mayana, live in SW Florida, where they raise their three young boys. If he's not chasing his boys around the beach, he works with people worldwide through his Life Coaching and Sober Coaching Business or on hope-filled content through videos and courses. He loves spending time with Jesus, praying for people, writing, reading, and wrestling with his boys.

You can reach out to Erik through his website for coaching and speaking engagements.

https://www.recoveringreality.com/

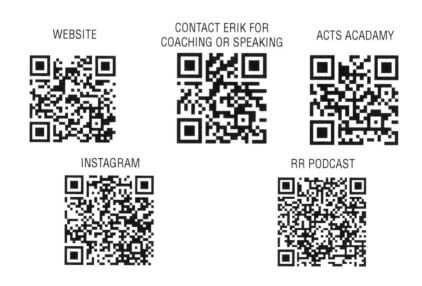

WEBSITE

CONTACT ERIK FOR
COACHING OR SPEAKING

ACTS ACADAMY

INSTAGRAM

RR PODCAST

Made in the USA
Columbia, SC
08 January 2025

49276614R00091